Simply Hemingway

Simply Hemingway

PETER L. HAYS

SIMPLY CHARLY
NEW YORK

Contents

Praise for *Simply Hemingway*

"A splendid introduction to Hemingway! With a seemingly effortless and graceful compression that Hemingway himself would have admired, Hays fits into this small package, Hemingway's outsized life and a critical overview of his extensive body of work. Hays writes with great expertise, with a strong sense of what is most important about Hemingway, and with an appreciation for current developments in the field. Here is a brief introduction to Hemingway for our times."

—Carl Eby, President of the Ernest Hemingway Foundation and Society

"'Know how complicated it is and then state it simply.' Life-long Hemingway scholar Peter Hays follows Hemingway's advice in this concise but thorough introduction to Hemingway's life and work. Hays knows how complex Hemingway's writing is and explains it simply and honestly, skillfully showing readers Hemingway's artistry and the lasting cultural significance of the iconic American modernist's literary legacy."

—Lisa Tyler, Editor of Wharton, Hemingway, *and the Advent of Modernism* and *Teaching Hemingway's* A Farewell to Arms

"Ernest Hemingway, a giant of 20th-century Modernist literature, has another biography, one that catches the complexity of Hemingway the man and the variety in his writing, the best and the flawed in a biography that can be read in an afternoon or an evening. Peter Hays, life-long Hemingway scholar, skilled teacher, was ideal for such a challenge."

—Joseph Flora, president emeritus, The Ernest Hemingway Foundation and Society

"Professor Hays has written a book for which I have long waited. It belongs on the Hemingway shelf of all local libraries as well as in all college and university libraries. Hays builds his book on the best in Hemingway scholarship over the years. He provides rich insight into the complexity that is both Hemingway's life and his works. It is written with grace and reads with ease. There is nothing simple about this fine short book. It is the best single-volume introduction to Hemingway we have."

—**Larry Grimes, coauthor of *Reading Hemingway's The Old Man and the Sea* and coeditor of *Hemingway, Cuba, and the Cuban Works***

"Fans of *The Sun Also Rises, The Old Man and the Sea,* and other totems of American literature have known for a half-century that Peter L. Hays is one of the secret weapons of Hemingway studies. Always exacting in his close readings yet creative in the topics he analyzes and the interpretive approaches he plies, he's always been such a stealth team player, we've taken his contributions for granted. *Simply Hemingway,* his entry in Simply Charly's *Great Lives* series, reminds us of how thoroughly Hays knows his subject and how fluidly and flawlessly he can narrate it. In essence, this concise biography goes down as easy as the Bollinger, Piper-Heidsieck, and Perrier-Jouët the writer himself loved to quaff (among many other beverages he loved to quaff). Hays does readers the great favor of giving equal attention to overlooked stories such as "The Old Man at the Bridge," "God Rest You Merry, Gentlemen," and "The Capital of the World" as he does the greatest hits that get all the love. He also doesn't commit the cardinal sin of treating the final two decades of the life as a depressing nonstop downward spiral. It's all here: the adventure and travel, the wars, wives, and wounds, but most of all, the brilliant writing Hemingway produced during his forty-year career. Hays tells it as succinctly and yet as dramatically as the author himself would."

—Kirk Curnutt, co-editor (with Suzanne del Gizzo), *The New Hemingway Studies*

Other *Great Lives*

Series Editor's Foreword

S imply Charly's "Great Lives" series offers brief but authoritative introductions to the world's most influential people—scientists, artists, writers, economists, and other historical figures whose contributions have had a meaningful and enduring impact on our society.

Each book provides an illuminating look at the works, ideas, personal lives, and the legacies these individuals left behind, also shedding light on the thought processes, specific events, and experiences that led these remarkable people to their groundbreaking discoveries or other achievements. Additionally, every volume explores various challenges they had to face and overcome to make history in their respective fields, as well as the little-known character traits, quirks, strengths, and frailties, myths, and controversies that sometimes surrounded these personalities.

Our authors are prominent scholars and other top experts who have dedicated their careers to exploring each facet of their subjects' work and personal lives.

Unlike many other works that are merely descriptions of the major milestones in a person's life, the "Great Lives" series goes above and beyond the standard format and content. It brings substance, depth, and clarity to the sometimes-complex lives and works of history's most powerful and influential people.

We hope that by exploring this series, readers will not only gain new knowledge and understanding of what drove these geniuses, but also find inspiration for their own lives. Isn't this what a great book is supposed to do?

Charles Carlini, Simply Charly
New York City

Preface

My first publication on Ernest Hemingway (July 21, 1899–July 2, 1961) was in 1965 when I was still a graduate student; I also published that year on William Styron and continued to publish on other authors as well. I did not concentrate on Hemingway for 20 years until the chair of my department told me I should specialize if I wanted to be promoted further. Having just returned from a Hemingway International Conference on the sunny Adriatic Coast of Italy, with a side trip to Venice, and in the company of friendly and generous people, I decided to make Hemingway my central research interest. I appreciated his terse style, the implied but unstated, which left room for interpretation, and the essentially Existentialist philosophy, that life is a matter of choices and living up to them. I do not regret choosing this research topic. However, the more I learned, the more complex Hemingway became.

I wish to dispel the many myths that have accrued around this great American writer; many of which he created himself. Whatever comfort he got from appearing hyper-masculine, the image also helped to sell books. He created a larger-than-life figure—boxer, lover, hunter, fisherman, writer—and when he couldn't live up to that heroic but false image, he ended his life. However, all these myths were rooted in facts, historical and artistic.

Hemingway came of age at the beginning of the 20th century, as America emerged from World War I and as modernism swept the art world. He took part in three wars—WWI, the Spanish Civil War, and World War II—either as a participant or as an observer; sometimes both. And he created a style that has influenced later generations of writers, initially a sparse style that implied much more than it stated and depended upon engaged readers for full comprehension. After *Men Without Women* in 1927, his style became more relaxed, especially in his novels, telling more than had previously only been suggested. He never—in his lifetime—wrote two of the same kind of novel.

In the Introduction, I explore Hemingway's formative years, his home life, and the things that formed him—both inborn and acquired. Then, in subsequent chapters, I detail his life and writing accomplishments, roughly decade by decade, analyzing some of the major works. Some periods, like the 1920s and 1930s, saw enormous amounts of publication, while the 1940s saw very little—the war was only partly to blame. Another prominent American novelist of that era, F. Scott Fitzgerald, said that Hemingway needed a new woman for each book, and it largely worked out that way: Hadley Richardson for *The Sun Also Rises*, Pauline Pfeiffer for *A Farewell to Arms*, Martha Gellhorn for *For Whom the Bell Tolls*, Adriana Ivancich for *Across the River and Into the Trees* and *The Old Man and the Sea*, and Mary Welsh for *A Moveable Feast*.

Periods of great creativity were frequently followed by less productive times, where hunting, fishing, and letter writing prevailed over the creation of fiction (but Hemingway sometimes also fictionalized his life in his letters). It's natural to want to relax after any major effort, but bursts of energy followed by lassitude also fit a pattern of bipolar condition, although Hemingway never exhibited full mania; his life cycle, until the 1954 plane crashes, seem more cyclothymic: milder highs and not quite-as-deep lows, unlike those of usual bipolar depressive disorder. However, Hemingway never received an accurate psychiatric evaluation when he was at the Mayo Clinic in 1960-61, before his suicide—initially his doctor felt that his depression was a side effect of a blood-pressure medication he was taking. But after stopping that medication and electric shock therapy, and a second visit to the clinic with more of the same treatment, he was still depressive and suicidal, and a better diagnosis was not reached—or never to this day announced. Nevertheless, Hemingway kept writing, struggling at the end to bring shape to numerous unfinished works that would be published, posthumously, and edited by other hands, such as *Moveable Feast*, *The Garden of Eden*, *Islands in the Stream*, *The Dangerous Summer*, and two versions of his African journal, *True at First Light* and *Under Kilimanjaro.*

I will first focus on Hemingway, and then on each of these works, in the pages that follow.

I. Introduction

E rnest Hemingway was a very complicated man; there was nothing simple about him. For years, he had a hypermasculine image: hard drinker, hunter, big game fisherman, lover of many women, boxer, and misogynist. But those who knew him contradict that assessment, describing him as an extremely shy person who was unsure of himself. Yet, his contemporary, American poet and writer Archibald MacLeish said that his self-confidence was such that "no one sucked oxygen out of a room" like Hemingway, except for President Franklin Delano Roosevelt.

In his early 20s and living in France, Hemingway convinced other literary expatriates—poet Ezra Pound and Gertrude Stein, whose Paris home was a famous meeting spot for the leading artists of the time—that he had talent worth developing. He cheated on at least his first three wives, and physically and verbally abused his fourth; and yet women in Sun Valley, Idaho, where the writer lived intermittently later in his life, said that he organized shoots, made sure that language was clean, and that the women had first shots at the ducks or other game birds. Though at times he was a macho blusterer, Honoria Murphy, the last survivor of a famed family of American expatriates in 1920s France, remembered him as "the most gentle and loveliest man I have ever known. When he came to see Patrick [her teenage brother] as he lay dying [of tuberculosis], Hemingway wept openly. It was the first time I had ever seen a grown man cry." At different times, for different people, he was a different man.

Oak Park childhood

Born on July 21, 1899, into a middle-class family of Clarence and Grace Hemingway, in Oak Park, a suburb of Chicago that he characterized later as having wide lawns and narrow minds, young Ernest had a largely untroubled and happy childhood. He had an elder sister, Marcelline, three younger ones (Ursula, Carol, and Madelaine), and a brother, Leicester, born when he was 15. The family spent each summer on Walloon Lake in northern Michigan, near Petoskey, where Ernest's father taught him to hunt and fish, activities that he reveled in and that he brought home to the Des Plaines River, just west of Oak Park. The family also bought and operated a farm across Walloon Lake from their cottage, Windemere. Ernest graduated from Oak Park High School, having played cello in the orchestra, second-string guard on the football team, and serving as captain of the water polo team. He also wrote for the school's newspaper and literary magazine, contributing three short stories, two of which are an imitation of Jack London's work. There is no record of any serious high school romances.

Unlike Marcelline, who went to Oberlin College as had his father, Ernest joined the Kansas City *Star* as a cub reporter in the fall of 1917, just months after the US had joined WWI. He worked at the *Star* only six and a half months, but he learned to get the facts of a story and to deliver it with evocative details. In the spring of 1918, Ernest joined the Red Cross as an ambulance driver in Italy, where, in July, he was seriously wounded. He fell in love with his nurse, Agnes von Kurowsky, seven years his senior. He went back to the States after recuperating, waited for Agnes to join him, but instead got a "Dear John" letter from her. He went back to Michigan for the summer and fall, then Toronto in January 1920 as the companion of a crippled boy whose parents he had met in Petoskey. While in Canada, he began contributing to the Toronto *Star*. He returned to Oak Park briefly in May, then went back to Michigan for the summer. In June, when Ernest was 21, his actions caused a disagreement with his mother: he hosted a late-night party with some teenage girls, including his sisters. His mother threw him out. Ernest went back to Chicago to get a new job on a cooperative society publication.

Complicating what was largely an idyllic youth was a mental illness he likely inherited from his father (who committed suicide, as did Ernest and at least two of his siblings and one granddaughter). Two of his sons had electroshock therapy, as did he, and one granddaughter is institutionalized. He was an alcoholic, and he probably suffered from Post-Traumatic Stress Disorder (PTSD) as well. He also suffered multiple injuries, which included concussions (chronic traumatic encephalopathy), starting with being blown up at 18 while serving as a Red Cross volunteer in Italy during WWI. Later, in WWII, he was driven into a water tower in London during a blackout, sustaining a head wound that required 57 stitches to close. Still later, he was in two plane crashes in two days in Africa, which may have included a fractured skull. These last injuries hastened his decline into dementia and paranoia, but he still struggled to write, working on the manuscripts that became his posthumous works.

When *Garden of Eden* was published posthumously in 1986, it created a reevaluation of Hemingway's macho image. Its characters' gender-bending behavior and sexual experimentation added to what had been found in Hemingway's documents and letters, housed in the John F. Kennedy Library in Boston, which opened in 1980, and in Mary Hemingway's autobiography, *How It Was* (1976). Besides dyeing his hair on occasion, Ernest wrote in Mary's diary an imagined interview: Reporter: "Mr. Hemingway, is it true that your wife is a lesbian?" Papa: "Of course not. Mrs. Hemingway is a boy." Reporter: "What are your favorite sports, sir?" Papa: "Shooting, fishing, reading and sodomy'" (425). He also wrote there that Mary "loves me to be her girls, which I love to be" (426).

The trove of documents in the presidential library revealed that Hemingway's mother had twinned him with his older sister, keeping him in dresses and long curls beyond the age when most boys would start wearing pants. That led to a spate of books, including Kenneth Lynn's 1987 biography *Hemingway*; Mark Spilka's *Hemingway's Quarrel with Androgyny* (1990), and later, Carl Eby's *Hemingway's Fetishism* (1999) and Debra Moddelmog's *Reading Desire* (1999) that questioned whether Hemingway had developed a firm gender identity as a child. It may be that the macho pose was an attempt to be indisputably masculine and also to cover the sensitive artist within, to convince the world—and even himself—that he was, as he boasted as a child, "fraid a nothing."

Critics pointed out that the narrator's portrayals of the female characters in "Up in Michigan" and "Hills Like White Elephants" are more sympathetic than his portrayal of the male characters; they noticed his discussion of homosexuality in "A Simple Enquiry," "The Sea Change," "A Lack of Passion," and in *To Have and Have Not.* So while the macho image lingers in the popular imagination, in criticism it has been replaced by a more complicated vision, one that looks at questions of gender, race, class, and ecology, as well as at the artistic means by which he achieved his effects.

In addition to genetics, there was his home life. His mother was a trained contralto who received a contract from the New York Metropolitan Opera Company. She declined it because the arc lights hurt her eyes. She went back to Oak Park and married physician Clarence Ed Hemingway. They lived initially with her father, Ernest Hall, and throughout her life, she used her full name, Grace Hall Hemingway, when few women did. She charged $8 an hour for voice lessons, when a laboring man might make a dollar a day, and often earned $1000 a month, while Dr. Ed initially made $50 a month; later, his practice grew, specializing in obstetrics. Ed was tall and strong, a skilled hunter and fisherman, a naturalist who formed an Agassiz Club (a society founded for the study of natural science) for youths of the neighborhood, and trained his son to be an acute observer. Ed often supplied his family with game for meals, but he also did much of the cooking at Oak Park, and most of the baking as well. Grace, with her income, felt justified in hiring housemaids, although she did cook at their vacation home at Walloon Lake. Both parents were devout. Grace directed the choir at the Congregational Church they attended. Ed was a teetotaler all his life; Grace, more artistic and social, insisted, over Ed's objections, that all six children have music and dancing lessons and go to dances. Thus, in addition to being initially twinned with his older sister Marcelline, Ernest saw a strange dynamic in his own household: a mother who made more money than his father, a mother who overrode his father's religious scruples, although both were pietistic and sent back to the publishers his books as obscene. He had a hunter/fisherman for a father, a physician, bearded and strong, but who also did the cooking and canning. Ed also had notoriously shifting moods: happy and joking one moment, a stern, strap-wielding disciplinarian the next—signs likely of his bipolar illness.

Anti-Romantic content, seemingly simple style

After his family, the most impressive life-forming experience was the war—and falling in love with his nurse, Agnes, who later jilted him. Both sides of World War I had propaganda arms, furthering each side's cause. Britain had ads of the War Secretary, Lord Kitchener, pointing a finger directly at the viewer and saying, "Your country needs you." The United States soon followed suit with an ad of Uncle Sam pointing at the viewer, saying, "I want you for the U.S. Army." Patriotism, romanticism, and dreams of military glory were used to convince young men (and women as nurses) to join the war machine. Wilfred Owen, an English poet who was killed in France one week before the war ended in 1918, wrote a poem titled "Dulce et Decorum Est" (sweet and fitting it is to die for one's country). Owen concluded the poem, a blistering description of life and death in the trenches, with a searing portrait of a soldier choking to death on poison gas, "My friend, you would not tell with such high zest/ To children ardent for some desperate glory, / The old Lie: *Dulce et decorum est/ Pro patria mori.*"

Hemingway tried to enlist, but his poor vision in his left eye kept him out (and he was too vain to wear glasses). After high school, he joined the Kansas City *Star* as a cub reporter, but after less than seven months there, he joined the Red Cross as an ambulance driver, though he was only 18 at the time. His first task in Italy, before arriving at his assigned post, was to pick up dead bodies, and scraps of bodies—many of them women—after a munitions plant blew up outside Milan. At Fossalta di Piave, a town near Venice, he was handing out chocolate and cigarettes as part of a Red Cross canteen. Two weeks before his 19th birthday, on July 8, 1918, a forward listening post he was visiting—such posts were set up to get early warnings of enemy movements—was struck by a trench mortar shell, essentially a five-gallon can filled with scrap metal. The man in between him and the blast was immediately killed. Ernest sustained major injuries: at the hospital, 227 shell fragments and two machine-gun bullets were removed from his right leg, but luckily there were no major wounds to the upper torso and only minor ones to the hands. He spent four months recuperating and regaining the use of his legs—although still limping. He went back to the front for one day, where he was diagnosed with jaundice, and finished the war in the hospital in Milan. He only spent five weeks on active duty, but he saw no glory, no fitting way to die for one's country. As he wrote in A *Farewell to Arms* (1929), "I was always embarrassed by the words sacred, glory, and sacrifice.... I had seen nothing sacred, and the things that were glorious had no glory and the sacrifices were like the stockyards of Chicago if nothing was done with the meat except to bury it."

Hemingway was part of a movement that came back from the war, disbelieving what the propaganda machines had cranked out and what romantic nostalgia echoed. These included Wilfred Owen, Siegfried Sassoon, Robert Graves, Frederic Manning, and non-veteran D. H. Lawrence in England. In the U.S., there was poet e. e. cummings and novelist John Dos Passos, as well as Hemingway—all ambulance drivers, all harsh critics of the war. F. Scott Fitzgerald, who served but never left the United States, concluded his first novel by saying his generation had "grown up to find all Gods dead, all wars fought, all faiths in man shaken" (*This Side of Paradise*). Gertrude Stein called these veterans the "Lost Generation." The writers built on the movement of realism that had begun in the late 19th century with Mark Twain and William Dean Howells. But no one went to the bathroom in these gentlemen's novels; sexual attraction might be alluded to but never directly mentioned. Prudery reigned, and it was felt that nothing should be published that brought a blush to a young lady's face. The naturalists of the 1880s and 90s—including Frank Norris and Stephen Crane—attacked these restrictions, and after WWI, more disaffected authors became truth-tellers who denied such Victorian pieties as Robert Browning's "God's in his Heaven/All's right with the world!" More particularly, for Hemingway, anti-Romantic that he was, there was W. E. Henley's "Invictus," the poem that ends with, "I am the master of my fate,/ I am the captain of my soul."

Hemingway, blown up while delivering chocolate, knew he wasn't the master of his fate. Who lived and who died seemed a matter of chance, luck, accident, but certainly not personal will. How one reacted to what fate handed out, however, was within one's control. And thus, yes, one could be the captain of one's soul. Hemingway's universe was dark. His characters usually lose. Yet he drew them in such a way that we are asked to admire their stoicism, their self-control, their dedication, and their dignity. In *The Old Man and the Sea*, Santiago is towed to sea by a huge fish he fights with for days, only to lose it to sharks on his return to port. As Hemingway wrote, "A man can be destroyed but not defeated"; he asked us to judge people by their commitment to their self-definition and to their art rather than their successes—whether it be fishing, bullfighting, boxing, or writing. They may be destroyed by fate, but they are not defeated if they maintain their integrity and dedication to their own values, as we shall see in several stories. Twenty years before French philosophers Albert Camus and Jean-Paul Sartre, Hemingway had us judge characters by the existential choices they made.

Hemingway's fame rests on a wonderful collection of short stories, three major novels, and one novella, and a change in the way fiction is written. Mark Twain, whose use of dialogue in *The Adventures of Huckleberry Finn* Hemingway admired and imitated, used lengthy sentences in other books, as this narrator's description of Dawson's Landing in *Pudd'nhead Wilson* (1893) demonstrates: "Each of these pretty homes had a garden in front. Fenced with white palings and opulently stocked with hollyhocks, marigolds, touch-me-nots, prince's-feathers, and other old-fashioned flowers; while on the window-sills of the houses stood wooden boxes containing moss-rose plants and terra-cotta pots in which grew a breed of geranium whose spread of intensely red blossoms accented the prevailing pink tint of the rose-clad house-front like an explosion of flame"—59 words in the second sentence, which rambles on like roses. Henry James' *The Ambassadors* (1903), which I have just opened at random, has sentences like these: "He was conscious of how much it was affected, this sense, by something subdued and discreet in the way she had arranged herself for her special object and her morning walk—he believed her to have come on foot; the way her slightly thicker veil was drawn—a mere touch, but everything; the composed gravity of her dress, in which, here and there, a dull winecolour seemed to gleam faintly through the black, the charming discretion of her small, compact head; the quiet note, as she sat, of her folded, gray-gloved hands." Ninety-two words, embedded clauses, and phrases. By the time Hemingway published, automobiles were common; so were airplanes and movies. Radio was beginning as a source of entertainment. Families no longer watched stereopticon slides or sat in the parlor while father read pages from the Bible or a novel suitable for the whole family. The pace of life had quickened dramatically after WWI, with Prohibition and speakeasies, the Jazz Age and the Charleston, the shimmy, and the Black Bottom, and women's hemlines rising off the floor. The Victorian Age had ended, and the era of mechanization had begun. Hemingway provided a shorter, more direct, more masculine style. Here is his description of a woman: "Brett was damn good-looking. She wore a slipover jersey sweater and a tweed skirt, and her hair was brushed back like a boy's." Five words and then 19; average: 12 words a sentence. The style of composition that is now taught in college English courses is much more Hemingway than it is Henry James, or even Mark Twain in his descriptive passages.

After having been told by Charles Dickens to "weep for Little

Nell" (*The Old Curiosity Shop*), as many Victorian writers directed their readers, and having been told by propaganda to enlist in the war, Hemingway eschewed editorial comment. He presented the circumstances of his characters. What those circumstances mean, and sometimes even their feelings, are left to the reader to infer. Hemingway changed how stories are told, but more of that later. He became an iconic figure of masculinity in the 1950s, is still advertised in furniture lines, among other commercial ventures, and appears in other people's fiction and over 120 comics. He became a cultural institution.

2. Becoming a Writer

After his return from WWI and being jilted by Agnes, Hemingway spent part of 1919 in Toronto as a young man's companion and a reporter for the Toronto *Star*. In the summer of that year, he went again to Walloon Lake and Petoskey, writing derivative adventure stories that no one would publish. He returned to Chicago, worked as writer and editor of a journal of the cooperative movement, the *Cooperative Commonwealth*, met writer Sherwood Anderson, and met, and then married, Hadley Richardson, eight years his senior and possessing a $3000 annual income. On Anderson's advice, and with his letters of introduction to Gertrude Stein and Ezra Pound, Hemingway abandoned plans to return to Italy, and instead, the couple moved to Paris in December 1921.

There, the modernist art capital of the world, Hemingway soon met Stein, Pound, English novelist and editor Ford Madox Ford, and Irish novelist James Joyce. At 22, with nothing substantial published, he convinced these authors that he possessed talent and submitted his manuscripts to them for advice and editing. Pound told him to beware of adjectives, to "use no superfluous word," and that "the natural object was always the *adequate* symbol." Stein, too, advised him to simplify his writing; both echoing the style sheet for the Kansas City *Star*, which told its reporters to "use short sentences. Use short first paragraphs. Use vigorous English..."—the style that Hemingway adopted. He brought one story from Illinois with him, "Up in Michigan," the first date-rape story in American fiction, although it was not published in the United States until 1938. That first year in Paris he also wrote a story in Sherwood Anderson's style and subject matter, "My Old Man," a first-person narration by a boy who learns at the time of his father's death in a racing accident that father, a jockey, has been involved in fixed horse-races, thus losing his parent and his idealized conception of him at the same time. Both are tales of sadder-but-wiser initiation. Hemingway wrote brief, one-paragraph sketches of Parisian life as exercises, trying to get, as he put it in *Death in the Afternoon*, "the sequence of motion and fact that made the emotion." His prose in the stories he started to write at that time is spare, allusive, implying more than it states. It employs what he would later call his "iceberg principle": that only one-eighth of the story showed, while the remaining seven-eighths were submerged; that he could omit details which the reader would mentally supply and understand. It often succeeded, and critics are still teasing out possible implied strands.

During these early years in Paris, Hemingway worked as the Toronto *Star's* foreign correspondent, and in late 1922, while in Switzerland covering the Lausanne Peace Conference to settle the Greco-Turkish War—which he had earlier reported on for the paper—he invited Hadley to join him for skiing after the conference. He wanted to show off his writings to more senior, published correspondents, so Hadley packed all his manuscripts into a valise. However, it was stolen when she left the train compartment to buy a bottle of water. Short stories and the beginning of a novel were lost. All that survived were manuscripts of "Up in Michigan" and "My Old Man" being returned to him in the mail. Starting over, writing more stripped-down, more evocative, less announced vignettes and stories, and employing the allusive technique of T. S. Eliot in *The Waste Land*, Hemingway wrote a new story, "Out of Season." It is about a young couple fishing in Cortina, Italy, out of season, while their marriage is also out-of-sorts. Their guide is a drunken Italian war veteran who takes the husband to a muddy river by a waste dump—Hemingway's first use of the Arthurian Fisher King who had appeared in Eliot's poem. The trip is canceled because the husband has no lead as a weight with which to fish, and also lacks metal in his spine—and perhaps no lead in his pencil either. This story is one example where I don't think the iceberg principle works. Hemingway later said that the real-life older man on whom the guide character is based committed suicide when no further fishing ensued. I don't think there's enough substance in the story for such a conclusion, but it's an evocative beginning.

Hemingway continued to work on the brief, one-to-two paragraph vignettes of intense life. That July, at Gertrude Stein's encouragement, the Hemingways went to Spain to see their first bullfights, and he became a lifelong enthusiast, an *aficionado*, of *torero*, admiring the skill of a matador named Nicanor Villalta. In the early fall of 1923, with Hadley pregnant, they moved to Canada for the birth of John Hadley Nicanor, nicknamed Bumby. But before they left Spain, Hemingway submitted 18 of his brief vignettes to a newspaper friend Bill Bird and also oversaw the publication of his first book in Paris—essentially a pamphlet—*Three Stories and Ten Poems*: His neo-Thomist poem, as he called it, is

The Lord is my shepherd, I shall not want him for long

Or "The Age Demanded":

The age demanded that we sing
  And cut away our tongue.
  The age demanded that we flow
  And hammered in the bung.
  The age demanded that we dance
  And jammed us into iron pants.
  And in the end the age was handed
  The sort of shit that it demanded.

Neither of these poems is in *Three Stories and Ten Poems*, but they're short enough to quote and to show why poetry was not Hemingway's métier; they also show his decidedly anti-Romantic, realistic point of view, as does his fiction. The three stories in the pamphlet—only 300 copies were printed—were "Up in Michigan," because France did not have the same proscriptions about describing sex as America did, at least not in English, "My Old Man," and "Out of Season."

The three months spent in Toronto were entirely newspaper

work; Hemingway's editor frequently sent him out of town to cover stories, including to New York to interview British prime minister David Lloyd George, and while he was returning, Hadley gave birth to Bumby. The Hemingways broke their lease and sailed back to Paris in January 1924, but before leaving, almost as a Christmas present, Bill Bird sent copies of *in our time* (lower case intended), the hand-printed booklet of Hemingway's 18 vignettes. Again, 300 copies were printed, but the raised watermark visible behind the printing spoiled 130; there were only 170 clean copies. But Hemingway was now the author of two books, however slim their content, and the owner of a burgeoning reputation.

In Our Time

Back in Paris, with an apartment overlooking a sawmill, Hemingway gave up journalism and turned to writing short stories. That spring they flowed, and he wrote eight, possibly in a hypomanic burst of energy. He also acted as unpaid assistant editor to Ford Madox Ford's *the transatlantic review* (lower case intended here as well) and Ford accepted "Indian Camp," still a classic American short story. In the summer of 1924, the Hemingways went with a group of friends to the festival of St. Fermin in Pamplona, Spain. Ernest entered the amateur bullfights, facing steers with padded horns; one he bulldogged to the ground. They also fished in the nearby trout streams and had a wonderful time all together.

The first of what was to be his next volume of stories was "Indian Camp," told in free indirect discourse, primarily following young Nick Adams' point of view. A character by the same name is present in many of Hemingway's stories, and they appear to be a cumulative biography, to some extent paralleling Hemingway's own life. But some details contradict others, and so one cannot assume that "Nick Adams" is always the same character or that he is Ernest Hemingway's alter ego. In "Indian Camp," an Indian woman has been undergoing labor for three days due to a breech birth. Nick's father, Dr. Adams, is summoned to help, and he comes with his brother

George and young son Nick, who were with him on a fishing vacation; Nick is perhaps nine. They arrive at the Indian village, former logging huts now occupied by Indians who peel hemlock bark to send to local tanneries and leave the wood to rot, multiple signs of displacement of the Native people and of their poverty, as well as of ecological disaster. Without anesthesia or medical tools, Dr. Adams performs a caesarian with a jackknife, while his brother and three Indian men hold the screaming woman down; her husband, who had cut his foot badly with an axe three days before, lies in the bunk above her. Nick watches, initially fascinated, soon repulsed: "He did not watch. His curiosity had been gone for a long time." The operation over, the self-satisfied doctor finally looks at the husband, only to find that man, distraught at his wife's screams and his inability to help, has committed suicide, slicing his neck with a razor; Nick also sees the dead man and his open wound. The story ends with Nick and his father rowing back to their fishing camp, Nick's sense of his own mortality shaken but not broken: "The sun was coming up over the hills. A bass jumped, making a circle in the water.... In the early morning on the lake sitting in the stern of the boat with his father rowing, he felt quite sure that he would never die." What Hemingway omitted, but hanging there for the reader to discern, is the enormous psychological blow to Nick to see his father plunge a knife into the belly of a screaming woman while four men hold her down. And while Dr. Adams is a competent obstetrician, he flounders in answering Nick's questions about suicide and death. An added twist to the story is that Uncle George distributes cigars to the Indians who row them to their camp, arousing the possibility that he is the child's father, further emasculating the woman's husband, already a dispossessed Native American. It features both life and death, and the symbolism of that cycle is in the circle the bass makes in the water. The story begins in darkness and ends in daylight; it, too, is an initiation story like "Up in Michigan," which begins in daylight and ends in darkness and mist, with Liz's callous introduction to sex.

With his newly written short stories, Hemingway approached

American publishers, and through the help of Harold Loeb, Paris friend and tennis buddy, as well as humorist Donald Ogden Stewart, he received a contract to publish *In Our Time* from Boni and Liveright in the spring of 1925, as the Hemingways returned from skiing in Schruns, Austria. The volume featured all of Hemingway's new stories, as well as "My Old Man" and "Out of Season" from *Three Stories and Ten Poems*. Liveright refused "Up in Michigan" because of its explicit sexuality; the book would have been seized by postal inspectors as obscene. In its place, Hemingway substituted "The Battler," a story about a punch-drunk fighter Ad Francis and his African American companion Bugs; though the title seems to point at the boxer, it applies as well to young Nick Adams, now perhaps 16 or 17, and hoboing through life. Nick is knocked off a train he has been riding on by its brakeman and walks along the railroad track, with swamp on either side, a possible reference to *Pilgrim's Progress*, certainly an allusion to life's surrounding unpleasantries, and finds Ad alone in a clearing beside a fire.

Ad has a misshapen face from years of being pummeled and only one flattened ear. He tells Nick, "All you kids are tough," and Nick replies, "You got to be tough." As they talk, Bugs appears with the dinner he has bought in town: ham, eggs, and bread. Hemingway accurately portrays the racism and social dichotomies of the 1920s: he uses the language of the time, including the word "nigger," to refer to Bugs, and Bugs, though older, addresses white, teen-aged Nick as Mr. Adams and "the gentleman." When Nick, at Bugs' insistence, refuses to give Ad the knife with which Nick has been slicing bread, Ad challenges Nick, advances on him, and tells him he's going to get a beating. Before that can happen, Bugs knocks Ad out with a blackjack (pun by Hemingway intended). When Nick leaves, he is up the railway embankment and on the track before he realizes Bugs has given him a sandwich for his journey; the incident was so distressing that Nick experienced a momentary dissociation.

Bugs is Ad's friend, traveling the country with him; in this story, Nick has no friends. And although Hemingway pictures Bugs as extremely polite, addressing young Nick as his social superior, like

Melville's Babo in "Benito Cereno," he actually is in control of the situation and of the two white men. Finally, Bugs' care for Ad is extremely maternal: he shops and cooks for Ad, tells Ad not to let the egg run down his chin, picks Ad up after knocking him out, and "laid him down gently.... [And] smoothed the coat he had placed under the unconscious man's head." In all of this, there is a hint of homosexuality; as Bugs says of Ad, "I liked him." Another initiation tale for Nick, one in which there are worlds of darkness.

In Our Time also included "Soldier's Home," possibly the first PTSD story in American literature, and it concluded with another similar one, "Big Two-Hearted River." Nick gets off the train in Michigan's Upper Peninsula at Seney, burnt to the ground by forest fires. (Seney is on the Fox River, but Hemingway moved the locale to include the duality of Two-Hearted.) Nick is now a returned veteran of the World War, although the war is never mentioned. Our clues are the as-in-war destroyed town, Nick's khaki shirt, and his overreaction to events such as losing a fish. He is another Fisher King, and the destroyed landscape is part of his wasteland, although much of it is internal. The surviving grasshoppers are all black, to blend in with the charred land, and Nick wonders how long they will stay that way—a self-reflexive concern. On the first page of the story, Hemingway has Nick notice four times how the trout held themselves steady in the current at the bottom of the river; holding himself steady is what Nick seeks to do with this essentially occupational-therapy outing: a familiar, enjoyable task, one where the participant can control most events, one that brings a sense of achievement on completion. Nick hikes a long distance with a heavy pack, tires himself out so that he can nap without thinking; thinking, such as "why me," "why the dead," is not wanted. Eventually, he reaches a suitable campsite, sets up camp with great diligence and attention to detail, and very carefully makes dinner—again, controlling both his environment and himself. The next day, he overreacts on losing a fish—feels nauseous and must sit down—an event he could not control, then catches two more. The story concludes with Nick's determining that there are many days to come in which he can fish in the swamp—we're back to the iconography of "The Battler"—where fishing would be "tragic." In this context, "tragic" seems inappropriate, but for Nick, at this stage of his recovery, the uncontrollable is indeed tragic.

Hemingway combined the 16 short vignettes from *In Our Time* as Roman-numbered interchapters between the longer short stories he had just written; he included two of the 18 vignettes as short stories. Boni and Liveright brought the book out in October 1925 in a first printing of 1335 copies (while printing 2,000 copies of William Faulkner's *Soldier's Pay* in 1926). But short story collections sell less well than novels, and his publishers expected no large sales. They were right: the book sold only 642 copies by the end of 1925, but critics noticed it, and Hemingway was on his way.

A new woman and a first novel

In the spring of 1925, Loeb and his girlfriend Kitty Cannell introduced the Hemingways to Pauline Pfeiffer, a short, dark-haired, vivacious editor of Paris *Vogue*; like Hadley, she hailed from St. Louis. Pauline and Hadley became close friends, and she became a frequent visitor at the couple's home. Late that April, Hemingway met F. Scott Fitzgerald, who was writing his editor, Max Perkins, at Scribner's to keep an eye out for Hemingway. In the summer of 1925, Hemingway and Hadley went back to Pamplona and its bullfighting festival. They were accompanied by Loeb, British socialite Duff Twysden and her fiancé Pat Guthrie, Hemingway's Chicago friend Bill Smith, and Donald Ogden Stewart. Duff was an attractive woman; she and Loeb had spent a week together previously at St. Jean-de-Luz. Hemingway found her desirable, but Loeb and her fiancé were present; Ernest had Hadley there. Sexual tensions pervaded the group, at one point leading to a challenge to a fistfight between Loeb and Hemingway, a challenge not carried out and followed by an apology from Ernest. To further impinge on the joyousness of the vacation, the trout streams had been ruined by logging and were mud-clogged. It was a sad comedown from the previous summer's festivities, but it provided ample fodder for a novel, and Hemingway immediately began writing what would become *The Sun Also Rises*, finishing the first draft by late September.

He then set upon serious rewriting, fashioning the novel about the love of newspaperman Jake Barnes, a genitally wounded WWI veteran, for the promiscuous Lady Brett Ashley, the soon-to-be-divorced wife of a British baronet. Jake and Brett met when he was in hospital, and she was a nurses' aide; they love each other but cannot consummate their relationship. Her "own true love" died in the war; as a nurse, she treated the seriously wounded and likely developed PTSD; after the war, her PTSD-afflicted husband abused her. Both Jake and Brett have been wounded by the war, he physically, she emotionally. He was evidently wounded in the penis—the novel is discreet, but there's a poignant scene where Jake examines himself in a bedside mirror—but not the testicles; he has desires but cannot effectuate them. Now Brett seeks sexual satisfaction and monetary support from other men. This is a prime example of fate dealing one a poor hand, and our measure of how the individual who received that fate behaves. The first-person novel begins in Paris, where Jake's friends are Robert Cohn, middle-weight boxing champion at Princeton, a recently published author based on Harold Loeb, Robert's girlfriend Francis Clyne and Brett Ashley, based on Duff Twysden, as well as her fiancé Mike Campbell, a former British officer, drunkard and bankrupt (morally as well as financially), living on a small income and awaiting an inheritance. Hemingway used Campbell's bankruptcy, like Jake's impotence, as a continuing metaphor throughout the novel: the morals of many are bankrupt; the war caused them to lose faith in what they had believed; they are largely impotent in improving their lives; they are a Lost Generation.

Brett has short hair, "brushed back like a boy's," an androgynous name, wears men's hats, and arrogates to herself such formerly male prerogatives as smoking, drinking, and sleeping around. Other characters soon joining them in Paris are Jake's American friend, Bill Gorton, and Count Mippippolous, who picks up Brett and Jake at a Paris bar. A Greek businessman, wounded at age 21 in Abyssinia by arrows through his body, veteran of seven wars and four revolutions, he provides a model for Jake. He says, "it is because I have lived very much that now I can enjoy everything so well.... You must get to know the values" within life. That Jake must do. He arranges for all to go to Pamplona for the festival, preceding it with a fishing excursion to Burguete, in the foothills of the Pyrenees, for himself and Bill, accentuating his role as a maimed Fisher King. Nearby is the site of Roland's death as celebrated in the *Chanson de Roland*, but the age of romantic, epic heroes is long over. There, away from Brett and the sexual tensions she causes him, Jake sleeps more easily and confesses to Bill his love for her, receiving Bill's sympathy, implying that Bill knows of Jake's wound. Jake also reads A. E. W. Mason's "The Crystal Trench," about a man who waits beside a woman he silently loves while a glacier slowly moves to deposit her dead lover onto its moraine; the parallel is obvious. Cohn follows Brett to Pamplona, only to be insulted by Mike, who knows of their affair, and Mike's insults are blatantly anti-Semitic; Bill echoes them, and Hemingway has been accused of anti-Semitism in the book.

Meanwhile, Brett is attracted to a young, handsome matador, Pedro Romero, named for the 18th-century father of modern Spanish bullfighting, and based on Cayetano Ordóñez. Jake praises Romero's style in ways that Hemingway wanted to apply to his own writing: "always it was straight and pure and natural in line.... [H]e kept the absolute purity of line...." Brett meets Romero through Jake's introduction and seduces the boy. And unlike Cohn, Romero does not make a fool of himself in his desire for Brett. He possesses enormous self-control, whether in the arena or outside it; and self-control, particularly when it comes to Brett, is what Jake needs. On the night of the penultimate bullfight, Cohn asks Jake where Brett has gone; he answers, truthfully but ambiguously, "to bed." Cohn knocks Jake out and Mike down; he then beats up Romero.

Refusing to concede, Romero gets up each time he is knocked down, and when Cohn finally apologizes, Romero hits him with what little strength he has left. The next day, Romero fights magnificently: "The fight with Cohn had not touched his spirit but his face had been smashed and his body hurt. He was wiping all that out now." Romero is clearly the captain of his soul, the masculine icon in the novel. That night, he and Brett leave for Madrid together; Cohn has already left Pamplona for Paris.

After leaving Bill and Mike (who needs Bill to pay his bar tab), Jake goes to San Sebastian to recuperate from the fiesta (*Fiesta* is the title of the novel in Great Britain). He swims in the bay, a baptism of sorts, swimming down through the depths and up through the clearing water. Back at his hotel, there's a telegram from Brett in Madrid, asking for help. "That meant San Sebastian all shot to hell"—with reference to a traditional painting of St. Sebastian pierced by arrows. He replies, thinking: "Send a girl off with one man [Cohn]. Introduce her to another to go off with him [Romero]. Now go and bring her back. And sign the wire with love. That was it all right." The sarcasm is acid.

In Madrid, which Jake describes as "the end of the line,"—both of the railroad and his romance—Jake finds Brett alone, with the room in "that disorder produced only by those who have always had servants." Romero has left her, or she has made him go. He wanted her to be a conventional Spanish wife: "He wanted me to grow my hair out. Me. With long hair, I'd look so like hell.... He said it would make me look more womanly.... I'm thirty-four, you know. [Romero is nineteen.] I'm not going to be one of those bitches that ruins children." Jake finds that Romero has paid the hotel bill. He buys tickets to Paris for the two of them and takes Brett to lunch at Botín's restaurant, where he drinks heavily. He has decided that there is no point in pursuing Brett any further; despite his pleas, she will not live with him. But still, tearing himself away from her costs him emotionally. As they drive down the ironically named Gran Via (Grand Way), with Brett close beside him, she says, "Oh, Jake ... we could have had such a damned good time together." They pass a policeman holding up a baton, a reminder of what Jake cannot do, and Jake—ending the novel—says, out of his pain," Yes ... [i]sn't it pretty to think so."

The novel carried two epigraphs: Stein's "You are all a lost generation," and from Ecclesiastes, "One generation passeth away, and another generation cometh; but the earth abideth forever...." The first epigraph took most notice and the second was largely ignored. The novel was tagged as speaking for the Lost Generation, those who had come out of the war dispirited, drinking too much (despite Prohibition), and depressed; again, in Fitzgerald's words, "all Gods dead... all faiths in man shaken." Initial reviews frequently praised the style of the book, its vivid sentences, while decrying the characters, their drunkenness, and aimlessness. They ignored the second epigraph, which emphasized both continuity and the sun's rising, which gave the novel its title. The world goes on. It doesn't care about any of us, and therefore we have to learn to live in it with what fate has given us and live with self-control. That's Jake's dilemma (named for Jacob, who wrestled with an angel), and Hemingway portrayed it well.

Hemingway's contract with Boni and Liveright gave them rights to his next three books unless they refused publication of one. He was disappointed by the publishing firm's limited advertising of his book—and the small print run. He decided to break with Boni and Liveright, whose best-selling author at the time was Sherwood Anderson; his novel *Dark Laughter* sold 22,000 copies in 1925. So, in 10 days in November of that year, Hemingway wrote a parody of Anderson's novel, titling it, like Ivan Turgenev's 1872 novella, *Torrents of Spring*, with epigraphs to each chapter from Henry Fielding. It was funny for the in-crowd, those who knew of Anderson's novel and its mannerisms or of the Parisians Hemingway also mocked. Fitzgerald praised it, although one of his drunken episodes appears in the book with him named, but Hadley thought it an attack on an old friend; Pauline Pfeiffer, however, thought it very funny. When Ernest and Hadley returned to Austria for winter skiing, she joined them. And in late January 1926, on his way to

New York to switch publishers, Hemingway stopped in Paris to see Pauline.

Liveright would not accept a novel making fun of their current best-selling author, Anderson, and that broke Hemingway's contract with them. He had been corresponding with Maxwell Perkins at Scribners, Fitzgerald's publishers, and Scott had been urging Max to sign Hemingway. Scribners did, accepting *Torrents of Spring*, which they did not expect to sell much, and the yet unseen *The Sun Also Rises*. Concluding his business dealings, Hemingway went back to France, spending time with Pauline, before returning to Hadley and their son. Later that spring, Hadley learned of the affair between her husband and Pauline. She and Ernest separated, and she insisted on a hundred-day separation between the lovers before she would grant a divorce. Pauline went back home to Piggott, Arkansas, and Ernest moved into the Parisian painting studio of his friend, Gerald Murphy.

After Hemingway finalized *The Sun Also Rises*, he continued writing short stories for his next collection, beyond those already written after *In Our Time*. One advantage of being with Scribners was that they had their own magazine and could publish his short stories, paying him once for magazine publication and again for the story when in a book. The novel was published in October of 1926, selling 9350 copies by the end of the year, a good number for a first novel, with Hemingway assigning all royalties to Hadley. Scribners accepted three of Hemingway's new stories for its own magazine. He was now well on his way.

3. A Second Wife, A Second American Book of Stories

Hadley relented before the 100 days were up, granting Hemingway his divorce in late January 1927, and Pauline came back to Paris. Despite their affair, she was a devout Catholic and wanted Hemingway to convert to her faith and be married in the church. He went with a newspaperman friend back to Italy to find the priest who had given him extreme unction when he was wounded during the war, which would serve in lieu of baptism for becoming a Catholic. The trip revealed the extent to which Fascism and corruption had swept Italy under Benito Mussolini and became the basis of first a journalistic publication, and then a short story, "Che Ti Dice la Patria" (what is the homeland saying), one of a dozen stories in his next collection *Men Without Women*. It was so named because most of the stories focused exclusively on males—with one notable exception—because several were written while Hemingway was without either Hadley or Pauline looking after him.

Pauline was four years older than Hemingway—30 in 1927—and she was rich. Her uncle Gus owned much of Pfeiffer Chemicals, which merged with Lambert Pharmaceuticals, then Warner-Lambert, and now Pfizer. Gus and his wife were childless and doted on Pauline. Her father, who owned stock in the family chemical/pharmaceutical/cosmetic conglomerate as well, went into farming and owned 13,000 acres of land in northern Arkansas, where sharecroppers grew cotton for him. Pauline and Ernest married in May 1927 and honeymooned at le Grau du Roi, in the south of France (setting for the opening of *The Garden of Eden*), they rented an apartment at rue Férou, near the church of St. Sulpice, no longer a fourth-floor walkup or an apartment overlooking a sawmill. Ernest continued writing and rewriting short stories for *Men without Women*. He and Pauline went again to Spain that summer for the bullfights in Pamplona and Valencia, and then on to Santiago de Compostela. That October, *Men Without Women*, comprised of 14 stories, was published by Scribners.

The first, "The Undefeated," features Manuel Garcia, an aging *torero* fresh out of the hospital after having been gored in the leg in his one previous fight of the year. He pleads with Retana, the bullfight promoter who controls Madrid's arenas, to put him in the ring, and Retana grudgingly agrees to let Garcia appear as a substitute, after reducing by half what he had originally intended to pay him. Hemingway makes clear the commercialization of what was once a religious ceremony and was still, in the skill and practice of some bullfighters, an art form in which the bullfighter puts his life on the line; as Hemingway put it, it was "ballet with death at the end." It represented man against nature, man against death, with art and courage being the weapons.

Garcia goes to a café to meet an old friend, picador Zurito, and to ask him for help in bullfights; without a picador's skillful wounding of a bull to lower his head, the bullfighter's chances of killing the bull without being gored himself are much lower. Zurito agrees, making Garcia promise to quit if he fights badly. Their event follows the Charlotadas, bullfight burlesques in the manner of Charlie Chaplin movies. The bulls they will fight are either too old, too young, or too diseased to pass daylight inspection. Again, the artistic spectacle is debased. It was this commercialization and denigration which moved Hemingway to capture what remained of bullfighting in *Death in the Afternoon*.

In the story, Hemingway introduces a substitute newspaper bullfight critic, a ploy of his to enable us to judge one man's character in contradistinction to another's. The newspaper critic uses stale clichés to describe the fight, reports crowd reaction rather than his own supposedly expert judgment, and leaves the fight early because he has a date: "What the hell was it anyway? Only a nocturnal. If he missed anything, he would get it out of the morning papers." Told largely from Garcia's point of view, Hemingway shifts sometimes to that of the bull. He contrasts the newspaper critic's lack of dedication to his profession to Garcia's self-identification as a bullfighter and life-on-the-line commitment to it.

Garcia fights brilliantly. "Why, that one's a great bullfighter," his sword-handler, Retana's man says, "'No, he's not,' said Zurito." A bullfighter needs luck, and Garcia has none—only skill. Four times he tries to plunge the sword through the narrow opening of the shoulder blades, and four times he strikes bone and is knocked down, the last time gored through the chest after he trips on a cushion thrown from the stands by a disgruntled spectator. Despite that, he gets up and, on his fifth try, kills the bull, and is rushed immediately to the arena's infirmary. There, Zurito takes a pair of scissors to cut off Garcia's *coleta*, the pigtail that bullfighters wear, and Garcia sits up on the operating table to protest: "I was going good.... I didn't have any luck. That was all." Whether he survives the goring is left unanswered. And if he survives, will he fight again? Nevertheless, the title of the story identifies Garcia as undefeated. He has lived up to his self-definition. He has acquired skill through hard work and practice, and he has dedicated his life to exercising those skills in the performance of an art, as Hemingway also did. Garcia may be destroyed, but he is not defeated.

Four more stories of the 14 published in *Men Without Women* deserve to be discussed; it is an incredibly rich volume. One, "The Killers," was for years Hemingway's most anthologized story. It focuses on the 16- or 17-year-old Nick Adams at a former bar, now turned into a lunchroom during Prohibition, and a Petoskey, Michigan, setting, described as Summit, Illinois. While Nick is sitting at the counter one winter day, two small, overdressed men come in, order dinner, and then force Nick and the cook into the kitchen, where they are tied up. Conversing with George the counterman, the two men state that they intend to kill Ole Andresen, a boxer, "for a friend." Andresen does not come in and the killers depart, leaving Nick, the cook, and George alive; had Andresen come in and been killed, the three witnesses would also have been murdered. The cook, Sam, is Black, and he warns Nick not to get further involved, again showing Hemingway's awareness of the limited power African Americans felt in this country. But Nick, swaggering off the gag that had been in his mouth and wanting to be a hero, walks to Andresen's boarding house to warn him. Andresen knows he has been marked for death, that there is nothing Nick can do. The boxer just looks at the wall, resignedly, like Herman Melville's Bartleby. Nick returns to the diner, where George guesses that Andresen double-crossed some gamblers in a fixed contest, as in "My Old Man" and "Fifty Grand." Things are not what they seem in the story: the bar is a diner, its clock is fast, the dinner menu is not available, Mrs. Bell runs Mrs. Hirsch's boarding house, the imposing boxer is defenseless, and small men who look like a vaudeville team can be killers. George then tells Nick not to think about any of it, impossible advice, and Nick decides to leave town. But he can't escape evil by moving, and he can't be a hero easily. Another initiation tale.

A second story, "In Another Country," takes its title from Christopher Marlowe's *The Jew of Malta*, by way of T. S. Eliot's "Portrait of a Lady." (Unlike Eliot, Hemingway did not footnote his erudition, but it's there for readers to pick up.) The protagonist narrator is an unnamed WWI soldier who could easily be Nick Adams. He has been wounded in the leg and walks each day with other wounded soldiers to a hospital in Milan for physical therapy, as Hemingway also did. Most of the soldiers with whom he walks are legitimate heroes; he knows that the medals he received were primarily because he was an American fighting in Italy, and he fears going back into service, fearing that he will not act heroically. He is being treated, not for his sake, but so that he can serve again: he is part of the war machine, a part to be fixed and recycled. And the "fixing" is done by other machines, which have never been used before; the men are, in today's terms, the beta testers. The narrator has a stiff knee, which a machine tries repeatedly to bend. He sits next to a major, once a champion fencer, now with a deformed hand that is slapped by mechanical straps to restore strength and motion to the fingers. They both face photos of before and after industrial accidents where the machines fixed the injuries, but since they believe the machines are brand new, they regard the photos as propaganda.

Hemingway noted that the soldiers walk together through the sections of town where workers live and where Communism is rife, informing us that the war was not universally popular in Italy, especially not in poorer, working-class neighborhoods. Rarely overtly political, Hemingway nonetheless was a trained reporter, and he captured the political and social situation of his time, as well as the personal dilemmas of his characters.

The major chides the protagonist for his poor Italian grammar and insists that he perfect it. Despite disbelieving in the machines, he comes to the hospital daily; it gives his life order. He insists the protagonist learn grammar, another system of order—much as Nick systematically set up camp in "Big Two-Hearted River." One day the major breaks down, crying, telling the narrator, "A man must not marry.... He cannot marry." The narrator learns that the major's young wife, whom he did not marry until wounded in the war—i.e., not marrying her until he was sure not to leave her a widow—has just died of pneumonia, most likely from the Spanish flu epidemic. Yet on that day, the major still came to the hospital and continued to return, having only the hopeless hope of being cured, and his grammar, to sustain him.

Another war story is "Now I Lay Me," based on the child's prayer "Now I lay me down to sleep/ I pray the Lord my soul to keep. / If I die before I wake/ I pray the Lord my soul to take." This is a first-person Nick Adams story as he, a lieutenant in the Italian army, rests for the night seven kilometers behind the lines. He does not sleep, fearing that if he falls asleep in the darkness, the Lord will take his soul as he felt his soul leaving his body when wounded, contrary to the wish expressed in the prayer of the story's title. He listens to silkworms munching on mulberry leaves, possibly a *momento mori*, and he occupies himself by trying to remember every stream he ever fished in. Some details are exactly the same as those in "Big, Two-Hearted River," raising the metafictional possibility that "River" is not an account of an actual event but rather a figment of Nick's imagination. He also remembers his home life, starting with a desiccated, possibly moldy slice of his parents' wedding cake hanging in a tin in the attic, and continuing to his mother's repeated "cleanings." She burns jars of biological specimens her doctor husband has collected, and at another time burns his collection of Native American artifacts: arrowheads, stone axes, and pottery. At neither time does the doctor vocally remonstrate against the destruction of his property; he has been emasculated, underscored by the ruining of such phallic objects as the preserved snakes or the arrowheads.

Nick's orderly John wakens and the two talk, largely of John's wife and children in Chicago. John's concerns are that he never sees the lieutenant sleep, and his belief that Nick's problems would all be solved if he married, especially a rich Italian girl: "A man ought to be married. You'll never regret it. Every man ought to be married." But given the history of his parents' marriage, Nick has no such inclination, and he concludes the story saying, "[S]o far, I have never married."

The final story I wish to discuss from *Men Without Women* concerns a woman, and is now Hemingway's most anthologized story, "Hills Like White Elephants." The woman makes the comparison, saying that the hills in the distance have the color of white elephants; "white elephants," of course, is a name for unwanted gifts, and the unwanted gift in this story, for the man, is the woman's pregnancy. The couple discuss abortion, but the word "abortion" is never mentioned; if it had been, the story would have been pulled off news racks at the time as obscene. Its absence, the unseen part of the iceberg, necessitates reader involvement. The couple are tourists at a railway junction in Spain, waiting for a train to Madrid, but also at a junction in their relationship. If she has the baby, he will resent her and the child; if she has the abortion, she will resent him. Like "abortion," neither "child," "infant," or "baby" are ever mentioned; for the man, it is always "it," and the operation "is perfectly simple," "just to let the air in."

The woman stares at ripe fields of grain across the river from them, in contrast to the dry, sterile, treeless land behind them—the contrast of fertility and sterility is obvious. Besides the river, there are numerous barriers: language (the woman does not speak Spanish), a bead curtain separating them outside the bar from the bar itself—beads are suggestive of a rosary—and, most importantly, their attitudes. The man constantly, passive-aggressively pressures the woman to have the abortion. At one point, as the man walks through the bar, Hemingway shifts from objective narration into the man's point of view, as he regards all the people "waiting reasonably for the train"; the woman, by arguing, has been, in his opinion, unreasonable.

Hemingway carefully labels the two main characters: he is "the man"; she is "the girl." He is the man, presumably, because he speaks Spanish and has organized the trip, and presumably, it is his money they are traveling on. She is "the girl" because she lacks self-confidence, "Because," as she says, "I don't care about me." After their discussion, however, she says, "I feel fine.... There's nothing wrong with me. I feel fine." There is nothing wrong with being pregnant. And Hemingway has dropped "the girl"; now, she is "she." Whether she will get on the train with the man, get off in Madrid, and have the abortion, Hemingway leaves to the reader.

A new novel

Hemingway discarded a false start on a novel and began a new one, which like "In Another Country" and "Now I Lay Me," reached back to WWI; he had also pulled a skylight down on his head, causing the large scar visible on his forehead. Pauline was pregnant, and the Hemingways left France in the spring of 1928, arriving ultimately in Key West, Florida, where Hemingway alternated writing in the mornings and fishing in the afternoons. In May they went to Pauline's home in Piggott, to prepare for the birth of their first child, which happened in late June in Kansas City. Ernest took the two home to Piggott, then drove to Wyoming, away from his crying son Patrick, to alternate fishing and writing. He finished the first draft of A *Farewell to Arms* in late August.

The family returned to a rented home in Key West, and Hemingway worked on revising the novel. In December 1928, his father committed suicide; Ernest was on a train heading south after having picked up Bumby (who had arrived from Paris) in NY. Hemingway switched trains to go to Oak Park, leaving Bumby in the care of a train porter to travel on to Key West, while he went to make the funeral arrangements and to pay his family's exigent bills.

Scribners agreed to serialize A *Farewell to Arms* in its magazine, as Hemingway struggled to get the ending right; there are 47 extant versions. Both Perkins and the magazine's editor wanted Hemingway to remove obscenities and explicit sex scenes; he agreed to the substitution of dashes for the obscenities and omitting the sex scenes in the magazine—which was delivered through the mail—but not in the novel. He, Pauline, Bumby, and Patrick returned to France in April, and the first installment of the novel appeared in May 1929; the second installment of the magazine in June was deemed salacious and banned in Boston by the chief of police, despite the omissions of obscenities and sex scenes. The publicity about the ban stirred interest in the book and gave Perkins ammunition in his crusade for fewer objectionable words; after some argument, Perkins finally allowed the word "bedpan," but dashes remained elsewhere. Hemingway attended the bullfights in Spain that summer, and A *Farewell to Arms* was published in late September 1929 to excellent reviews and large sales.

The novel is the first-person narration of an American officer, Frederic Henry, of an Italian ambulance unit in Italy. Narcissistic, he is disappointed that the war has not shut down when he goes on leave, primarily to visit brothels throughout Italy. He meets and lusts after a British nurse, Catherine Barkley, whose fiancé died in the war, "blown to bits" in the battle of the Somme, and she, to pull herself from her depression—nurses also suffer PTSD—accepts Frederic as a curative love object. Their ensuing romance is like a dance where the male doesn't realize that his partner is actually doing the leading. She makes a home of all their lodgings: his hospital room, a hotel in which they spend the night, the inn in Switzerland to which they escape after he deserts. She teaches him empathy and how to love, and only after her death in childbirth does he realize how much he has lost; ostensibly his story, it is really a tribute to her. The title comes from the original title of George Peele's poem, "Farewell to Arms," now anthologized by its first line, "His golden locks time hath to silver turned," about Elizabeth I's champion retiring from the field; it also refers to the opening line of Virgil Aenied: "I sing of arms and the man." Henry loses both those arms, that of war, and those of his lover.

The first paragraph of the novel has justifiably received much scrutiny and praise. "In the late summer of that year [1915] we lived in a house in a village that looked across the river and the plain to the mountains.... Troops went by the house and down the road and the dust they raised powdered the leaves of the trees. The trunks of the trees too were dusty, and the leaves fell early that year...." Henry's description of the house anticipates Catherine's domesticity, and the dust from the troops on the trees suggests mortality, dust-to-dust, as the early autumn evokes the fall of man. The first brief chapter concludes: "There were mists over the river and clouds on the mountains and the trucks splashed mud on the road and the troops were wet and muddy under their capes; their rifles were wet and under their capes the two leather cartridge-boxes on the front of the belts ... bulged forward under the capes so that the men ... marched as though they were six months gone with child." They are pregnant with death, and the first chapter foretells the end of the novel. The last paragraph of the chapter: "At the start of winter came the permanent rain and with the rain came the cholera. But it was checked and in the end only seven thousand died of it in the army." Whether the narrator is being sarcastic or not, the number reminds us of how many died of disease in WWI and also how those running the war considered loss of life necessary to gain even minimal territory. The sentences read with the rhythm of prose poetry, with the recurring symbol of rain—which Catherine fears—and the ominous presence of death.

When Caporetto falls after a battle in late 1917—Hemingway was still in high school in 1917—the Italian army has to retreat, and Henry has to take his ambulances, loaded with medical equipment, to safety. Avoiding main roads for fear they would be bombed—as they were—he uses country roads and gets stuck in the mud. He shoots an infantry sergeant who refuses to help him push his stuck ambulance, loses his vehicles, and gradually his men as well: one gets shot by nervous, defending Italian forces; another deserts. Stopped at a bridge across the Tagliamento River, where officers are being shot for not leading their men to victory—an impossibility under the circumstances—and where Henry, speaking Italian with an accent could be accused of being a spy, he deserts, diving into the river. He makes his way back to Milan, finds that Catherine has gone to Stresa on Lake Maggiore, and meets her there for a romantic reunion. Warned that he will be questioned, he and Catherine row the length of the lake into neutral Switzerland and sanctuary. After an idyllic stay in the mountains, they descend to Lausanne for the birth of their child. Catherine, after a long labor, has a caesarian (based on Pauline's), hemorrhages, and dies, as does their son, strangled by his umbilical cord. And like so many Hemingway protagonists, Henry is left alone.

Hemingway's bitter philosophy is well expressed in the novel:

> If people bring so much courage to this world, the world has to kill them to break them, so of course it kills them. The world breaks every one and afterward many are strong at the broken places. But those that will not break it kills.
>
> That was what you did. You died. You did not know what it was about. You never had time to learn. They threw you in and told you the rules and the first time they caught you off base they killed you.

Nevertheless, Henry has also learned the lesson of love from Catherine, and the novel sold well and might have continued so if sales were not limited by the Great Depression, which struck the following month. Nevertheless, Laurence Stallings, Marine veteran author of *What Price Glory*, penned a stage adaptation, which failed, and Hollywood produced a film version, starring Gary Cooper and Helen Hayes.

4. Half-day Fishing, Half-day Writing, Bone Break, & Bullfighting

T he Hemingways returned to another rented Key West house in January 1930. Before leaving Paris, Ernest had written a long article for *Fortune* magazine, where Archie MacLeish was an editor, on "Bullfighting, Sport and Industry," for which *Fortune* paid him $1000 (worth $15,582 in 2021). It was the beginning of his next book, one he had talked about for years: an explanation of bullfighting for an English-speaking audience, an analysis of the condition of Spanish bullfighting under an increasingly commercialized situation, a survey of current and past bullfighters, complete with photographs, and a glossary of Spanish terms. It also included comments on literature, such as on his contemporary William Faulkner's work, and art in general: Hemingway was linking his writing to bullfighting as two crafts, two arts. Work on the book alternated with fishing in the Gulf of Mexico, as far as the Dry Tortugas, and then in the summer, when Key West got too hot, he went back to Wyoming. Fishing and writing then alternated with hunting bear, mountain sheep, and elk. Scribners bought the rights to *In Our Time* from Boni Liveright, and Ernest made changes to two stories: changing the nurse's name from Ag (as in Agnes von Kurowsky) to Luz and the place names in "A Very Short Story" in order to make the story less autobiographical and restored some of the material Harold Liveright had thought too sexually explicit in "Mr. and Mrs. Elliott." Hemingway wrote a brief piece, which he called "An Introduction by the Author," describing horrific scenes of the evacuation of Greek women from Smyrna—there were no men; they were all at war. This short piece accurately sets the tone for Hemingway's view that there was no peace at that time. The book also had an introduction by literary critic Edmund Wilson. Scribners brought out the book in October 1930 to modest sales—5000 copies by year's end.

In late August 1930, Hemingway's horse bolted through thick woods, and Ernest suffered cuts to arms, legs, and his face; the face wound was sewn up in Cody, WY, by a former veterinarian become MD, with prescribed whiskey (as it was still in the time of Prohibition) as the only anesthetic. Despite the lacerations, he was involved in planning for an African safari, one to be paid for by Pauline's Uncle Gus. That trip, and completion of *Death in the Afternoon*, for which he already had over 200 manuscript pages, would be delayed. On November 1, coming back from Yellowstone National Park with John Dos Passos and another man, Hemingway was forced off the road into a ditch, their convertible overturning, pinning Hemingway's up-flung right arm against the open roof of the car; the arm sustained a spiral fracture just above the elbow.

They brought him to St. Vincent's Hospital in Billings, Montana. The fracture could not be set, and so the doctor operated and sutured the ends of the two bones together. Hemingway was placed in a cast and told not to move, lest he disrupt the healing of the bones. He was in the hospital six weeks, largely and impatiently immobile, getting out just before Christmas. He couldn't write; Pauline typed his letters by dictation. The only story he got from the incident was a largely true account, "The Gambler, the Nun, and the Radio." Both book-in-progress and safari were delayed. Upon discharge, he and Pauline returned to the Pfeiffer home in Piggott, Arkansas, and in the spring back to Key West, where Hemingway continued to exercise his arm with fishing trips in the Gulf; he also traveled to the Tortugas. Before they left for Spain in May so that Ernest could finish his bullfighting book with the latest data and photos, Uncle Gus bought them a house in Key West on 906 Whitehead Street (and it had no cats, six-toed or otherwise).

Ernest worked on the book that summer in Spain, while attending bullfights, and acquiring photos to use as illustrations. It was the time of the Second Spanish Republic, the deposition of the king, and an attempt at land reform in the country. With Pauline pregnant again, the Hemingways returned to New York in September, where Ernest conferred with Max Perkins about the book. Hemingway had over 100 photos; using them all would have made the book prohibitively expensive, especially during the Depression. He and Pauline moved in October to Kansas City to await the birth of their child; while there, Hemingway continued to revise *Death in the Afternoon*. Son Gregory was born November 12, 1931, and the family moved back to Key West, to a house undergoing refurbishing. Hemingway sent Scribners the manuscript in mid-January, postponed the planned African safari for another year, and turned again to writing short stories for a collection to follow *Death in the Afternoon*. By April 1932, he had discovered Cuba, renting rumrunner Joe Russell's boat, *Anita*, and had also discovered marlin fishing, a passion he pursued for years afterwards. In the summer, the Hemingways returned to northern Wyoming for fishing and hunting, and Ernest corrected page proofs for *Death in the Afternoon*. Scribners would have run parts of chapters of the book serially in its magazine, but Hemingway declined, saying that the chapters were whole units and he did not want them cut up. Because it was the Depression and the cost of reproducing photos would affect the cost of the book, Perkins and Hemingway went back and forth over the number and placement of photos. Hemingway wanted 112; he finally accepted 81, printed not as separate illustrations throughout the text but grouped together near the end. The book was published in September and sold for $3.50 ($60.00 today); it sold 10,000 copies by the end of 1932, one-quarter of the sales of A *Farewell to Arms*. Most Depression-era Americans simply weren't interested in bullfights.

Third American book of stories

During the spring and summer of 1933, Hemingway fished off Cuba and continued to work on the short stories that would be collected in *Winner Takes Nothing*, a title he composed from a book of gaming he made up, whose rules he said indicated that "the winner shall take nothing; neither his ease, nor his pleasure, nor any notions of glory, nor, if he win far enough, shall there be any reward within himself." The title, the invented quote, and many of the stories expressed Hemingway's dark view of life and of the world. *Winner Take Nothing* was published in October 1932 with 14 fourteen stories. It begins with "After the Storm," a story that Hemingway heard from one of his fishing guides, about a sunken liner and the guide's fruitless efforts to swim down to the wreck and appropriate what he could, including the jewels of a drowned woman who was visible through a porthole. It included "A Natural History of the Dead," lifted from *Death in the Afternoon*, in which Hemingway again insisted, as he did in *A Farewell to Arms*, that dying has no glory. Three significant stories are "A Clean Well-Lighted Place," "God Rest You Merry, Gentlemen," and "Fathers and Sons."

In "A Clean Well-Lighted Place," two waiters stay well into the night as an old, deaf man drinks alone "in the shadow leaves of the tree made against the electric light" on the patio of a café. Identified only as the younger and older waiters, the younger is anxious to get home to his wife and their bed. He insults the old man, who doesn't hear because of his deafness, and closes early. The older waiter sympathizes with the old man's plight: his loneliness—his wife is dead; his despair—he attempted suicide by hanging but was cut down by his niece; and his desire to sit in a quiet, attractive place and drink quietly. For the older waiter, all is "a nothing that he knew too well. It was all a nothing and a man was nothing too." As with Samuel Beckett later, "nothing" here is complete nothingness, no reason to live, no God or prior code. The waiter then blasphemes the Lord's Prayer and the Hail Mary: "Our nada [nothing] who art in nada, nada be thy name.... Hail nothing full of nothing, nothing is with thee." (Franco banished the story from Spain for its irreligiosity.) The older waiter tells himself that he only has insomnia, that many must have it, but what bothers him is existential despair—no reason to live except whatever people invent for themselves—and perhaps more than a touch of depression, which Hemingway also felt. From his early 20s on, his letters mention thoughts of suicide.

"God Rest You Merry, Gentlemen" came from a physician in Kansas City who ran a medical advice column in newspapers; Hemingway took the basic facts and moved them back to 1918 when he was a cub reporter in the city covering the hospital beat. The story concerns a religious teen, concerned that his normal sexual urges and spontaneous erections are sins against purity and signs of unholy lust. He comes to the hospital and begs the two doctors on call, Wilcox and Fischer, to castrate him to cure his problem. They refuse: Wilcox, who is generally incompetent, has been drinking and uses the *Young Doctor's Friend and Guide* to relate symptoms to treatment; he is also curt and dismissive. He tells the boy to leave and—the printed text has a dash; the manuscript reveals he wants the boy to "jack off." Fischer, in contrast, tries to tell the boy that his feelings are a normal part of growing up, that "what you complain of is no sinful state but the means of consummating a sacrament." Since they refuse to do what he wants, the boy leaves and, on Christmas, not knowing what castration is, amputates his penis with a straight razor. When the boy is brought to the hospital, Wilcox has difficulty stanching the flow of blood, and the boy may die.

The story is narrated by a young reporter whom Fischer nicknames Horace, probably for newspaperman Horace Greeley, and Fischer greets him with "What news along the Rialto?", a line from *The Merchant of Venice*, whose main character, Shylock, is a Jew, as is Fischer. As Hemingway also knew, over the main entrance to Kansas City's General Hospital were inscribed the words from Portia's speech in the same play: "The quality of mercy is not strained,/ It droppeth as the gentle rain from heaven/ Upon the place beneath." Wilcox, the Christian (and the second syllable of his name echoes the organ of the boy's concern), shows no mercy or charity on Christmas; Fischer, the Jew, and outsider, does show compassion—and he had previously lost a job on the coast for his willingness to oblige and bend statutes, presumably for the same reason. We have again a Fisher King situation: a young man on a quest, someone genitally wounded (here the young man himself), and a fisher, to the extent he can, of men. He also says that he has had, like Christ, a brief glimpse into hell. Wilcox asks Fischer not to tease him about the boy and continues to insist on Christmas day that Fischer is not a Christian, to which Fischer responds, "So good of you to remind me. Your *Saviour.* That's right. *Your* Saviour, undoubtedly *your* Saviour—and the ride for Palm Sunday." By which he means Wilcox is the ass on which Jesus rode on Palm Sunday.

The story is an attack on religious fanaticism and, echoing *The Merchant of Venice*, against antisemitism, perhaps a lessening of Hemingway's own. It includes his subtle erudition, combining Shakespeare, the Fisher King myth, and the Bible. And there is nothing to rest merry on, whether on Christmas or any other day in Hemingway's world.

The final story in *Winner Take Nothing* is "Fathers and Sons"; it would remain the last, the culminating story in the collected short stories five years later. It builds on an autobiographical reminiscence: Hemingway driving nine-year-old Bumby from Key West to Piggott to be with his half-brothers. Nick Adams is driving through red clay cotton country in the fall with his French-educated child asleep on the car seat beside him. It is the Depression, as Nick thinks of the inability of a town he's driving through to keep up payment on their traffic light. The story is told in stream of consciousness from Nick's point of view, Hemingway silently acknowledging the criticism that he continued largely to write in the same simple, declarative sentences of *In Our Time* and showing that he could do otherwise. As he drives through fields, Nick mentally hunts them, seeking where birds would find cover. The thoughts of hunting remind him of his father, who taught him how to hunt, and of his father's extremely sharp vision, like an eagle's. Nick also reflects on his father's suicide, indirectly reported, and of the trap of his home life—in which Nick participated. One striking image is of an eagle whose talons were caught in the canvas coverings of a duck decoy, as Nick's eagle-eyed father had been caught in a domestic trap that we have seen in "The Doctor and the Doctor's Wife" and "Now I Lay Me."

Nick's father was a sound mentor on hunting, a sadly deficit one on matters of sex: "masturbation produced blindness, insanity, and death, while a man who went with prostitutes would contract hideous venereal diseases and that the thing to do was to keep your hands off people." Dr. Adams also told young Nick that mashing "is one of the most heinous of crimes," which does not deter young Nick from thinking of "doing something, strange, bizarre, and heinous with a potato masher to a beautiful lady who looked like the picture of Anna Held on the inside of cigar boxes." These thoughts lead to Nick's memories of his own first sexual experiences with Trudy Gilby, a young Indian girl in the forest near his summer home. Young Nick also exhibits racial discrimination where it's all right for him to have sex with an Indian girl, but inappropriate for Trudy's elder brother to desire Nick's sister.

Bumby, unnamed in the story, awakes and asks his father what was it like to be with the Indians, but Nick is evasive and nearly as reticent as his father had been. The boy says, in the French tradition, that they should visit the tomb of his grandfather, which Hemingway does here virtually in the story: there is a reconciliation with his father in this fictional account of remembering, contrition, apology, and appreciation.

To Africa

Hemingway began a business relationship with Arnold Gingrich of *Esquire* magazine and sent him the first of many nonfiction pieces about fishing, hunting, and general observations that summer of 1933. He and Pauline spent late summer and early fall in Spain and Paris, before going to Africa on the safari Pauline's uncle Gus was paying for. *Winner Take Nothing* was published in October in a run of 20,300 copies, but only some 13,000 sold the first year. For many people, spending money on luxuries like fiction was out of the question. For the critics, many of whom were leftists, the country's plight was due to its economic system, and any author of worth would be criticizing that system, as Hemingway's friend John Dos Passos was doing. That Hemingway did not do so showed he was irrelevant, as demonstrated by the paucity of reviews that the book received. In response to that criticism, he wrote a long short story, "One Trip Across," about a Key West fishing boat captain Harry Morgan, named after a 17th-century Caribbean pirate, who is cheated out of charter money and reparations for lost gear. Struggling to make a living for his family, Harry agrees during the violent last days of the Machado's rule in Cuba to smuggle Chinese from Cuba into the US, but instead strangles the Chinese man who arranged for the venture and keeps the proffered money. Although Hemingway initially resisted open economic criticism, he obviously moved in that direction with "One Trip Across," and he was always experimenting with style. A *Farewell to Arms* is more discursive than *The Sun Also Rises*, while "Fathers and Sons," as well as other stories, use the stream-of-consciousness style.

In November 1933, the Hemingways and their Key West friend Charles Thompson sailed to Africa to meet their guide, Philip Percival, who had been the guide and white hunter for Hemingway's early hero, Teddy Roosevelt, during the president's African safari. The next three months were taken with shooting large game—lions, leopards, rhinos, Cape buffalo, but never elephants—and various species of gazelles and antelopes. They hunted in what was then Tanganyika and the Serengeti Plain in Tanzania. At one point, Hemingway, suffering seriously from amoebic dysentery, had to be flown to Nairobi for treatment. The safari provided the basis for his next book of non-fiction and for two of his best short stories. He and Pauline returned to Paris in March and then to New York City. Before returning to Key West, Hemingway ordered a 38-foot boat from Wheeler Shipyards in Brooklyn, the *Pilar* (Pauline's nickname) for $7500; he would pay for it, after the down payment, with his non-fiction contributions to *Esquire*, one of which he had already sent from Africa. That April, *Cosmopolitan* paid him $5500 ($106,000 today) to publish "One Trip Across."

Back in Key West that month, he began recounting his African trip in what became *Green Hills of Africa*. Hemingway inserted a forward notice: "The writer has attempted to write an absolutely true book to see whether the shape of a country and the pattern of a month's action can, if truly presented, compete with a work of the imagination." It may be the first non-fiction novel in American literature. And, as Hemingway noted, it focuses on the last month's hunting, as he and Charles Thompson, named Karl in the book, are in competition for the largest kudu head. The book individualizes the native servants and trackers, while still using racial stereotypes and observing the effects of British colonialism. It also comments on both literature and ecological history. Hemingway tells a Viennese labor contractor that America destroys its authors: "First, economically. They make money.... [T]hen our writers when they have made some money increase their standard of living and they are caught. They have to write to keep up their establishment, their wives, and so on, and they write slop.... Or else they read the critics. If they believe the critics when they say they are great then they must believe them when they say they are rotten and they lose confidence." One of those Hemingway had in mind was F. Scott Fitzgerald. Hemingway took the economic argument to heart, as we will see in "The Snows of Kilimanjaro." And the critical argument as well: he showed he could alter his style with a two-page single sentence, replete with italicized stream of consciousness (70-71). Ecologically, he wrote that "A country ages quickly once we come. The natives live in harmony with it. But the foreigner destroys, cuts down trees, drains water so that the water supply is altered and in a short time the soil, once the sod is turned under, is cropped out and next, it starts to blow away" as it was doing in the US Midwest then (as portrayed in John Steinbeck's *Grapes of Wrath*). "Our people went to America because it was a good place to go then. It had been a good country and we had made a bloody mess of it and I would go, now, somewhere else and as we had always gone." But while the land suffers, art endures: "A country, finally, erodes and the dust blows away, the people all die, and none of them were of any importance permanently except those who practiced the arts.... A work of art endures forever."

The book was serialized in Scribners magazine from May through November 1935 with illustrations by Edward Shenton; Hemingway had photographs, but didn't want *Green Hills of Africa* regarded as a travel book, but as a "true account" of actual experience. It was published as a book, with Shenton's drawings, in late October 1935 and never sold its first two printings in its first two years; one leftist reviewer wrote that Hemingway should write about strikes, not safaris. And, in a way, he did. On September 2, 1935, a massive hurricane hit Upper and Lower Matecumbe Keys, north of Key West. It destroyed the town of Islamorada as well as the camps of WWI veterans, employed by the Federal Emergency Relief Administration for $45 a month, building the Overseas Highway from Miami to Key West, and nearly 500 veterans and civilians were drowned. Hemingway sailed to the Matecumbe Keys to look for survivors and found only corpses, including those of two women operating a snack shack. He wrote an indignant opinion piece for the Communist Party's *New Masses* denouncing the Roosevelt administration for ignoring its own government weather warnings, not evacuating the veterans, and leaving them to drown.

Later that year, Hemingway returned to Harry Morgan and wrote a second story, this time about rum-running from Cuba, in which Harry gets shot in the arm and eventually loses it; he based part of the experience on his own seriously broken arm. Harry also loses his boat when it's identified by a government official as a smuggling vessel. The stories eventually grew into the novel *To Have and Have Not*. Other stories started that fall and published in periodicals the following year were "The Capital of the World (June 1936)," "Snows of Kilimanjaro" (August 1936), and "The Short Happy Life of Francis Macomber" (September of that year). In April, in his account of fishing for *Esquire*, he related the germ of what would become *The*

Old Man and the Sea, a paragraph about a Cuban fisherman towed to sea by a large marlin, only to have sharks strip the fish from him.

In July, the Spanish Civil War broke out, but Hemingway did not immediately go to observe and write about it; instead, he went back to northern Wyoming for hunting and fishing. While there, he continued to work on *To Have and Have Not,* adding a third Harry Morgan story about Cuban revolutionaries who rob a Key West bank and have Harry take them to Cuba, after they shoot his deckhand, Albert. Hemingway also adds a writer, Richard Gordon, based somewhat on John Dos Passos, as one who writes proletarian novels—based on his imagination. The writer sees Harry's wife, completely misreads her, and puts her into his novel-in-progress, just as she later sees him and misreads him. Gordon has been cheating on his wife with a beautiful socialite, one of the haves; as they are in bed, the woman's husband walks in, observes, and walks out. Gordon cannot finish, and the woman slaps him. Gordon's wife, Helen, complains of his infidelity and that "Love is just another dirty lie. Love is ergoapiol pills to make me come around because you were afraid to have a baby. Love is quinine and quinine and quinine until I'm deaf with it. Love is that dirty aborting horror that you took me to."

Harry shoots the four robbers but is shot himself, and as he and boat are towed by the Coast Guard back to Key West, Hemingway portrays a roomful of drunken, fighting WWI veterans working on government relief projects. Then at the end, he contrasts these have-nots with the rich on their yachts: a homosexual man and his now unwilling lover, an impotent tax-cheat lying alone on his bed, a Hollywood wife of a cirrhotic director who masturbates because her boyfriend didn't satisfy her and is now drunk and asleep, and the luminol she took isn't working fast enough to put her to sleep. Harry's final words are "No matter how a man alone ain't got a bloody fucking chance." Hemingway belatedly announced that he was joining the socially conscious, but the statement lacked artistic conviction. There is no daily picture of the life of the working poor. Harry, a former Miami police officer, owns a boat, a house, and a piano. He could fish to support his wife and three daughters; there are other venues for him than smuggling. But instead of ending on a proletarian note, Hemingway has Albert's wife pushed into the boat basin by those eager to see what the Coast Guard is bringing in, and in the water, she loses her dental plate. When rescued, she shouts, "Basards! Bishes!... Alber. Whersh Alber?" The movie *To Have and Have Not* with Humphrey Bogart and Lauren Bacall uses only Harry's name and that of the deckhand from "One Trip Across." It was completely rewritten by Jules Furthman and William Faulkner and has only a minimal relationship to Hemingway's novel, beyond the title.

War in Spain and a new woman

But before finishing the book, Hemingway had other things on his mind—the Spanish Civil War. He paid for ambulances for the Loyalists, and at that time a new woman, Martha Gellhorn, came into his life. Martha, her mother, and her brother visited Key West in December 1936. It was not a chance meeting: she had had a picture of Hemingway up in her dorm room at Bryn Mawr and she took her mother and brother to the bar he was known to frequent. When mother and brother left, Martha, a long-legged, lovely blonde of 28 and already a published author, stayed until mid-January. She and Hemingway met in Miami, as Hemingway was on his way to New York. There, he signed a contract with the North American News Alliance to write articles about the Spanish Civil War. In February, he joined with Dos Passos, Lillian Hellman, and Archibald MacLeish in forming a group to fund a movie about the war, which would be filmed by Communist Joris Ivens. Late that month he sailed for Europe, with Paris his first stop. The Allied Nations—France, Great Britain, and America—had declared neutrality in the war and blockaded Spain to prevent shipment of armaments from their nations. Meanwhile, Hitler used Spain as a laboratory for military tactics, flying squadrons of German planes and pilots to that country; Mussolini sent Italian troops, tanks, and planes to fight on Franco's side. Hemingway finally flew into Madrid in March 1937, and Martha soon joined him as a *Collier's* correspondent. At that time, Hemingway broke with Dos Passos over the execution of Dos Passos's friend and translator, José Robles, who had been killed by internecine communist conflicts. Hemingway believed the lie that Robles had been a traitor, and that sundered the friendship. Meanwhile, Martha had become his lover.

The film, *The Spanish Earth*, was finished in late April; Hemingway left Spain, spent a brief time in Paris, and sailed for New York in mid-May. He returned to Key West to continue work on *To Have and Have Not* and on the narrative for the Spanish film. He returned to New York briefly in June to deliver a speech before the Writers' Congress, denouncing fascism; while there, he also met with F. Scott Fitzgerald. In June, he replaced Orson Welles as the narrator of the film, which was shown at the White House in July, with Hemingway and Gellhorn present, as Eleanor Roosevelt was a fan of Gellhorn's writing. Subsequently, Hemingway flew to California with Ivens, hoping the film would raise money in Hollywood for the Loyalists (the Republican cause). They raised enough to purchase 20 ambulances. Back in New York, Hemingway read final proof of the novel, its flaws uncorrected, and prepared to return to Spain. He was in Spain that fall, watching a besieged Madrid when *To Have and Have Not* came out in late October. Although it sold well, it received deservedly poor reviews. The social criticism at its end was tacked on and was not well integrated.

A story he had begun about Loyalist counterespionage now took the form of a three-act melodrama, *The Fifth Column*. The title refers to the Rebel spies within Madrid, the fifth column joining the four military ones under Franco's control, advancing on Madrid. Its protagonist, Philip Rawlings, is an intelligence officer for the Republicans, masquerading as a hard-living journalist. He becomes the lover of a beautiful but uninformed blonde American journalist, Dorothy Bridges, based somewhat on Martha Gellhorn. As Gellhorn did, Dorothy uses her American money to buy a silver fox fur piece from a starving Madrileña (a female resident of the city). After some James Bond-like derring-do, Rawlings has to decide whether to leave Spain and go off or stay and commit himself to the fight against fascism. He leaves her, for "where I go now I go alone, or with others who go there for the same reason I go." He tells her "you're useless, really. You're uneducated. You're useless, you're a fool and you're lazy." He retracts the useless because of the sex they have enjoyed, then calls it a commodity he can't afford. (The play was subsequently produced in New York in 1940, rewritten by Benjamin Glazer, directed by Lee Strasberg, starring Franchot Tone and Lee J. Cobb. It ran for only 87 performances.)

Collected stories, some new and wonderful

Ernest left Spain just after Christmas 1937 and returned to Key West with Pauline, who had come to Europe to save their marriage. But the stay in the US was brief. By late March the following year, Hemingway was back in France, and by April in Spain, and reunited with Martha. By May, the couple came to Paris together and Hemingway returned to Key West to work on a just-begun novel and some stories. He and Perkins had debated including the play with his collected stories, and finally decided to do so. The collection, now titled *The Fifth Column and the First Forty-Nine Stories*, included the play, all of Hemingway's previously published stories plus "Up in Michigan," now publishable, and one brief Spanish war story, about an old man, separated from his animals on Easter Sunday, fleeing Rebel troops north across the Ebro River toward Barcelona. The goats were left behind, but the cat will be all right, the narrator tells the old man, and the doves will fly from their open cage. "It was a gray overcast day with a low ceiling so their [the Fascists'] planes were not up. That and the fact that cats know how to look after themselves was all the good luck the old man would ever have."

Another story in the collection is "The Capital of the World," about a naïve young Spanish boy from the provinces, Paco, working as a waiter in a Madrid boarding house. He is an admirer of three failing bullfighters who live there, one selling his highly decorated bullfighting suits to pay his rent. Two provincial priests also stay there, waiting in vain to see their respective bishops. The Catholic Church was the largest landholder in Spain and strenuously opposed land reforms. When the Civil War broke out, they stood with Franco and the Fascists against the Republican government. In response to an anarchist fellow waiter, Paco said he "would like to be a good catholic, a revolutionary, and have a steady job like this, while, at the same time, being a bullfighter." Cleaning up after everyone leaves, he practices the bullfighting passes named veronicas with a napkin. The dishwasher, Enrique, tells him he would be afraid in the arena, as he, Enrique, had been. Paco says no, and Enrique binds kitchen knives to the leg of a chair to simulate horns of a bull. On a pass, Paco does not move back far enough, and a knife pierces his belly. While his sister shares her disappointment with other Madrileños over Greta Garbo's first talking picture, *Anna Christie*, because the actress wears former prostitute Christie's simple clothes, not gowns and furs, in Eugene O'Neill's dark play, Paco bleeds to death. "He died, as the Spanish phrase has it, full of illusions."

The story "Up in Michigan," which was finally published in the U.S., was begun in Chicago in 1921 and published in Paris in 1923 in *Three Stories and Ten Poems*. It tells of a naïve teenage girl, Liz Coates, who had a crush on the local blacksmith in the 1890s in Horton Bay, Michigan. The girl "liked it about his mustache. She liked it about how his white teeth shown when he smiled. She liked it very much that he didn't look like a blacksmith." That is, she likes the superficialities but has no knowledge of the real man, and she can't articulate her feelings beyond liking. Jim is described by the narrator as a predator: he fishes illegally and brings back three deer, only one of which is described as a buck. The girl is so shy that she doesn't ask her employer if she can borrow eggs and flour to make a cake for the men when they go off on a hunting trip; if she had, she might have received some motherly advice.

The story is replete with sexual puns, including the one in the title, and in such lines, as the dead deer were "stiff and hard." It is a young man's story. Returning from the hunt, the men drink whiskey copiously; Jim, the blacksmith, has four drinks on an empty stomach before dinner. Afterwards, he cups Liz's breasts as she sits in the kitchen, his erection poking her through the back of her ladder chair. He persuades her to walk with him to the dock on the lake, and there, despite her protests, he rapes her and falls asleep on top of her. Liz tries to shake him awake, fails, kisses him, and tucks her coat around him. Her name is Coates; she has given herself, both willingly and unwillingly, to him. Like young Nick Adams in "Indian Camp," whose sense of his own immortality was only shaken by what he had seen, Liz's sense of romance is similarly shaken but not destroyed. The story ends with "[a] cold mist was coming up through the woods from the bay." Like the Nick Adams' story in *In Our Time*, this story, too, is one of initiation into a dark world—Liz emerges sadder but wiser.

Two major stories in the collection are "The Short, Happy Life of Francis Macomber" and "The Snows of Kilimanjaro," both based on his African safari. In the first, Macomber is presented as a rich, young man, emasculated by Hemingway and cuckolded by his wife, Margot. Macomber has a feminine first name, knows about sex from books rather than experience, and is frightened by a lion. He lies awake hearing the lion roar and is nervous the next morning at his prospect of having to kill it. Hemingway presents the situation very much as performance anxiety: Francis is worried about how he will perform, raising his phallic weapon at the appropriate time; Margot, unaware of his fear, tells him he will do marvelously. At the hunt, Macomber merely wounds the lion, and when it charges, he flees from it, leaving the white hunter Wilson to kill it. That night, Margot sleeps with Wilson, the alpha male. The next day, they hunt Cape buffalo. Furious at Wilson, with his adrenalin up and no disturbing lion roar bothering him, Macomber, in a car with Wilson and Margot, chases buffalo across a bumpy plain. "[H]e could see the plunging hugeness of the bull...the wide boss of his horn and his outstretched, wide-nostrilled muzzle, and he was raising his rifle when Wilson shouted, 'Not from the car, you fool!' and he had no fear, only hatred of Wilson, while the brakes clamped on and the car skidded, plowing sideways to an almost stop and Wilson was out on one side and he on the other, stumbling as his feet hit the still speeding-by of the earth, and then he was shooting as the bull moved away, ... emptying his rifle at him as he moved steadily away, finally remembering to get his shots forward into the shoulder, and as he fumbled to reload, he saw the bull was down." An almost page-long sentence, one where the recurrent present participles capture the sense of speed of the scene, and far from the simple declarative sentences of In Our Time.

Macomber and Wilson kill the other two bulls, and Macomber "felt a drunken elation.... In his life he had never felt so good." His fear is gone. Entirely so. He will be a cuckold no longer. Then a gun-bearer announces that the first bull has gotten up and gone into brush. Margot expects a second flight in the face of a charging animal, but a now fearless Macomber holds his ground on the charging bull, shooting high and hitting the bull's horns each time until his last shot, into the bull's nose and thus his brain. Afraid, Margot, in a direct line with her husband and the bull, takes her rifle and shoots from the car, hitting Francis in the back of the head, killing him. Wilson asks her why she didn't poison him. "That's the way they do it in England." When she pleads, "Oh. Please stop it.... Please, please stop it," Wilson finally desists.

It's a story of control, of self and others. Initially, Macomber can't control himself, his fear, or his wife. Chasing the bulls in cars is illegal and gives Margot control over Wilson. His necessary testimony that the shooting was an accident gives him control over her. And though the text says clearly that "Mrs. Macomber, in the car, had shot *at* the buffalo with the 6.5 Mannlicher as it seemed about to gore her husband" (my emphasis), many commentators insist Margot intended to kill her husband. Others say she wanted to save him, perhaps to further indebt him to her. And others acknowledge the text but believe there are Freudian slips.

The other African story is "The Snows of Kilimanjaro." Hemingway provides an epigraph of a leopard found frozen near the peak of Kilimanjaro, the western summit named in Masai as "The House of God." The preserved leopard provides an obvious contrast to the protagonist, Harry, rotting from gangrene on the plain below. The leopard may also refer to the opening of Dante's *Inferno*. Harry was a writer, but now he is the husband of a rich woman; he's a gigolo who has moved on from one rich woman to another, leaving his craft behind. As such, Harry is consumed as much by self-loathing as he is by the infection in his leg, acquired by a thorn-scratch while trying to take a photograph—an absurd wound—and he vents that self-hatred as abuse on his wife, Helen. "'Love is a dunghill,' said Harry. 'And I'm the cock that gets on it to crow,'" he admits, acknowledging his lack of love for Helen and his use of sex and lies to live in luxury. Helen is a romantic, who says he can't die if he doesn't give up, a philosophy Hemingway had combatted his entire career. She also wonders why it has this happened to them, seeking logic in a world that Hemingway believed had none, hence his avoidance of causal connectors such as "therefore" and "because," using instead the temporal "and" most frequently.

In stream of consciousness flashbacks, italicized, Harry thinks of other occasions of death, linked by snow as on Kilimanjaro. Some we have seen before, such as the snow refugees fleeing from Turkey are being sent into mountains to freeze, skiing in Austria, WWI deaths, including a slow euthanasia by morphine, and taking by skis a mentally challenged boy to the sheriff for shooting a man who tried to take hay the boy was charged with protecting.

Hemingway uses what could have been over a half dozen short stories in these flashbacks. He includes subtle political criticism, such as remarking that the Greeks fleeing from Turkey were sent to freeze in Bulgaria by the League of Nations Peace Commissioner from Norway, who should have known snow, and who won a Nobel Peace Prize for his efforts. Hemingway also criticizes the Greek artillery officers who killed their own troops with friendly fire as "Constantine officers," implying that they got their positions through connections to the royal family and not through merit and ability.

Harry thinks, "He had seen the world change; not just the events ... and he had watched the people, but he had seen the subtler change, and he could remember how people were at different times. He had been in it and he had watched it and it was his duty to write of it, but now he never would." Harry employs the dilatory excuse of many writers: "Now he would never write the things he had saved to write until he knew enough to write them well. Well, he would not have to fail at trying to write them either." In particular, he had intended to write "about the very rich; that you were really not of them but a spy in their country.... But he would never do it because each day of not writing, of comfort, of being that which he despised, dulled his ability and softened his will to work so that, finally, he did no work at all." One such self-recrimination about not writing about the rich leads him to remember "poor Julian," who "had started a story once that began—'The very rich are different from you and me.'" These words begin Fitzgerald's "The Rich Boy," and Fitzgerald had been named in the magazine publication of "Snows"; at Fitzgerald and Perkins' urging, Hemingway changed the name for book publication. Obviously, some of these thoughts about living with the rich were Hemingway's own, married to a well-to-do wife, but unlike Harry, he wrote constantly.

There are multiple harbingers of death in the story, starting with vultures that wait on a tree beside the camp. Then there are hyenas that cross in the dark and cry in the night. Harry thinks death could also come as a puff of wind, an evil smell, two silent bicycle policemen, or a heavy weight on his chest. The end of the story, reminiscent of Ambrose Bierce's "Occurrence at Owl Creek Bridge," has Harry believing that after waking the next day, a plane has come to take him to Nairobi for medical care. Flying high over the plain, over herds of zebra and wildebeest and a cloud of locusts, the plane turns toward Kilimanjaro, "great, high, and unbelievably white in the sun....And then he knew that was where he was going." In actuality, Helen wakes in the night to find Harry dead. Whether Harry's deathbed confession to himself of his sins and his repentance, as well as his mental composition of stories are sufficient for his salvation, he dies believing so. Many critics disagree.

The Fifth Column and the First Forty-Nine Stories (even here alliteration) was published in October 1938 to poor reviews for the play but generally good reviews for the short stories; thereafter, the play was printed separately with four stories of the Spanish Civil War. The volume concluded a decade that had seen the publication of Death in the Afternoon, Winner Take Nothing, Green Hills of Africa, To Have and Have Not, and the omnibus collection, as well as numerous non-fiction contributions to Esquire, The New Masses, and Ken, a new magazine by Esquire's publisher, in which Hemingway urged the United States to end its neutrality regarding the Spanish Civil War lest it have to fight more than Mussolini and Franco; in another he predicted the outbreak of a war in Europe by the summer of 1939. He was off by a month. He worked on more Spanish war stories and one that burgeoned into the novel For Whom the Bell Tolls. In April of 1939, the month the Spanish Civil War ended, he separated from Pauline and moved to Cuba with Martha, who soon found what would be Hemingway's house for the next 20 years, the Finca Vigia.

5. A Blockbuster

The rest of 1939 was filled with completing *For Whom the Bell Tolls*. He met Martha in Havana, Cuba in April, and she found the Finca Vigia (Lookout Farm), which would be Hemingway's home for the next 20 years. While Ernest went fishing, Martha began fixing up what was a dilapidated house at her own expense. The novel in progress grew constantly, with only weekend, rather than daily fishing trips, and when the August heat grew uncomfortable, he left Martha and went again back to Wyoming with all three sons. They arrived at the L Bar T Ranch just as WWII broke out in Europe in September. Pauline joined Ernest and the boys in October.

Averell Harriman, chair of the Union Pacific railroad, had built the Sun Valley Resort in 1936 as a winter ski, summer fishing, and fall hunting vacation spot near Ketchum, Idaho, to increase train traffic in the northwest, but the Great Depression had limited visitors. To increase business, Harriman "comped"—provided free lodging—to celebrities to attract more customers. Two such free guests were Hemingway and actor Gary Cooper; they became hunting and fishing companions and good friends. Accepting Harriman's offer, Hemingway left the Wyoming ranch and Pauline later in October 1939 and moved to Sun Valley. Martha joined him in room 206 of the Sun Valley Lodge, where he worked that fall on *For Whom the Bell Tolls*, putting in all he had gained from his visits, both to the battlefronts and to Gaylord's Hotel, where the Communist high command was located. Ernest worked through early December, Martha leaving before then to cover the Russo-Finnish War in Finland. He returned to Key West in December, found Pauline gone, and moved to the Finca.

Hemingway had divided *A Farewell to Arms* into five books; it was his five-act tragedy, a Romeo and Juliet story, with the lovers not only star-crossed, but also blocked by the war. *For Whom the Bell Tolls* would be his epic. And it grew mightily, not being finished, despite work on it almost daily, until July 1940. Hemingway was a committed anti-Fascist. Political commentary he had published in a short-lived periodical, *Ken*, in 1938, denounced Hitler and Mussolini, and America's blockade of Spain. The Spanish Civil War was the first war where civilian populations were targeted as measures of psychological warfare: Guernica, a Basque town with no military value, was destroyed by German bombers, as depicted by Pablo Picasso in his famous painting of that name. Because the Allied blockade limited the Spanish Republican army's ability to get armaments, while Italy and Germany supplied the Fascist Rebels, the Loyalist Republicans turned to Russia. The only major organized opposition to Fascism in Europe was Communism, and many of the left-wing politicians and labor groups had Communist ties. Several of the Republican generals had Russian military training, and many Americans who went to fight, members of the Lincoln Battalion, went because they were anti-fascist or Communists—as were some of the literary critics who had complained throughout the 1930s that Hemingway had not written sufficiently social-conscious books. They expected him to condemn Franco and the fascists, and to paint a heroic picture of the Loyalist Republicans. He disappointed them: he painted a relatively true account of the war, and the atrocities committed on both sides.

For Whom the Bell Tolls

The title of the novel comes from John Donne's Meditation XVII:

> No man is an island entire of itself; every man is a piece of the continent, a part of the main; ... any man's death diminishes me, because I am involved in mankind. And therefore never send to know for whom the bell tolls; it tolls for thee.

Hemingway declared, as he had at the end of *To Have and Have Not*, for human solidarity and interdependence. The novel opens with American Robert Jordan, a former University of Montana Spanish instructor and now a volunteer with the Republican Loyalists, lying flat on his stomach in the Sierra de Guadarrama mountains, observing a post guarding a bridge. Because of his experience with road crews in Montana, blasting at mountains to make roads, the Loyalists use him as a dynamiter, wherever in the war that might take him. The basic plot is simple. Jordan must blow the bridge in three days, and to do that, he must link with a Loyalist guerrilla band in the mountains, those who will attack the guard posts on both ends of the bridge and provide cover while he places and then detonates the dynamite. Jordan has been led through the fascist lines by Anselmo, a fit 60-year. He is an avid hunter of animals but hates killing humans. He takes Jordan to the mountain band of Pablo, one of several small groups of Republican guerrillas hiding and fighting in the mountains. Pablo, once a fierce killer of fascists, has now sunk into drink, fear, and a touch of remorse. He wants nothing that will bring danger to himself and the few horses he has accumulated, as Jordan's action will, drawing scrutiny on them. Later, he will destroy Jordan's detonators as a way to prevent the attack and save himself and his band. While he drinks, taking over the band's control is Pablo's wife Pilar—literally, a pillar—a large and forceful woman, commanding not with a scepter but with a stirring spoon. Denouncing Pablo's cowardness, she proclaims that "I am for the bridge and against thee.... I am for the Republic.... And the Republic is for the bridge." Of gypsy blood and claiming second sight, Pilar reads Jordan's hand and sees death in it; yet she will work with him for the Republic to blow the bridge, even if it means her sacrificing herself and the entire band.

Jordan also meets Maria, the daughter of a town mayor, who, with his wife, was shot against a slaughterhouse wall by Falangists, a political party serving Franco and the Rebel Fascists. Maria had her head shaven and was gang-raped. Now her blonde hair is growing back (a tribute to Martha Gellhorn), and she is under Pilar's care and emerging from her traumatic experience. Her hair is described as "the golden brown of a grain field," with the hint of fertility that suggests. There is an immediate attraction on both sides, and Maria slips into Jordan's sleeping bag that first night. One might say that she commits herself to love and life after her trauma, as Catherine Barkley had done in A *Farewell to Arms*, but it is less credibly an act of adult commitment and more Hemingway's creation of a female object of male wish fulfillment. Still, Hemingway convincingly reestablished her essential innocence when, in the sleeping bag with Jordan that first night, she asks about kissing: "Where do the noses go? I always wondered where the noses would go." And where the early Hemingway eschewed adjectives and adverbs, the older writer piles them on. Jordan, holding Maria against him in the sleeping bag, feels "a long warm coolness, cool outside and warm within, long and light and closely holding, closely held, lonely, hollow-making with contours, happy-making, young and loving, and now warmly smooth with a hollowing, chest-aching, tight-held loneliness that was such that Robert Jordan felt he could not stand it...."

Jordan does finally blow the bridge, but is injured and presumably dies immediately after the novel's end, being shot while providing cover for Pilar, Maria, Pablo, and surviving members of the guerrilla band. The novel is complicated by flashbacks of Jordan's earlier engagements with the fascist Nationalists, including one where he shoots a wounded comrade-in-arms to prevent his being captured and tortured. Other flashbacks include Jordan's visits to the Madrid hotel, Gaylord's, headquarters of the Communist command. The novel is lengthened by Jordan's stream-of-consciousness, thoughts about his father's suicide—Hemingway acknowledging that of his own father—Jordan's increasing love for Maria, and how his visits to an area often bring death to those Republicans who have helped him.

An innovation in the novel is the style of address. Hemingway stylized the dialogue with "thees" and "thous," indicating both the difference in Spanish between the familiar and the formal, and his desire to have his reading audience know that the dialogue in the novel is spoken in Spanish, translated by the author, and told as it is in the third person. To some extent, this formality exoticizes the novel, moving it to a distant place for American readers, and with the language, to an older time. Similarly, while Hemingway was able to include Spanish obscenities, others he translated into English, substituting "obscenity" for the actual term, as in "I obscenity in the milk of thy tiredness," "obscenity" substituting for "shit." The "thees" and "thous" were not consistently used; "you" also appeared. But overall, Hemingway managed the dialogue to achieve remarkable and moving rhythms.

To help Maria's healing, Pilar fosters the girl's relationship with Jordan, for the remainder of the four days and three nights of the novel—the rest of Jordan's life. Again, as in previous Hemingway works, we are asked to measure dedication to a cause, here the noble one of fighting fascism, for both Jordan and Pilar, and not the outcome, and to live life to the fullest while one can. The book was begun after the Spanish Civil War had ended and before WWII began, but it was published in October 1940, a year after the war had started in Europe, and it was Hemingway's *cri de coeur* against fascism and against political gamesmanship that cost human life.

Pablo's death gauntlet

Among the most noted parts of the book are Pilar's description of the smell of death and her account of Pablo taking over their hometown at the start of the war. He begins by surrounding the military barracks, cutting the phone wires, and dynamiting the walls. Those soldiers not killed by the blast and subsequent attack, those who have surrendered, he executes with an officer's pistol, after being instructed by one of the soldiers as to how to cock it. "Never have I fired a pistol," he said. The peasants on the Republican side had shotguns, fowling-pieces, against German-supplied Mauser rifles on the Nationalist Rebel side, rifles with considerably more range than shotguns, giving the Rebels enormous tactical advantage, as well as the trained military troops that Franco brought from North Africa and that Mussolini sent from Italy. After the successful attack on the barracks, Pablo rounds up all the rich in town—the landowners, store owners—as belonging to the Fascist Party, and the Catholic priest.

Pablo does not shoot them; instead, he organizes a gauntlet, with townsmen with flails, clubs, ox-goads, and wooden pitchforks, "to save bullets ... [a]nd that each man should have his share of the responsibility." It will be a socialist republic, with all things shared, land and guilt. The fascists walk through the line, are beaten, some to death, others only wounded, but all are then thrown over a cliff at the end of the row of men. The event is sordid, yet gripping, including a concluding scene where those who haven't yet exited the *Ayuntamiento*, the city hall, are set upon by the mob. Pilar describes the scene, looking through a window, standing on a chair outside the building:

> I saw the hall full of men flailing away with clubs and striking with flails and poking and striking and pushing and heaving against people with white wooden pitchforks that were now red and with their tines broken.... [A]nd men were screaming as horses scream in a fire. And I saw the priest with his skirts tucked up scrambling over a bench and those after him were chopping at him with sickles and reaping hooks....

Besides the Republicans, Loyalist peasants who have greater or lesser political awareness and involvement, the mob also includes anarchists who belong to neither the Republicans nor the Nationalist Rebels, who want no government whatsoever, and many of whom simply get drunk. Pilar tells Jordan and Maria, "[T]hat was the worst day of my life until one other day." That worst day was "Three days later when the fascists [returned and] took the town," and executed all the Republicans who could not get away.

Pilar lived with several bullfighters before Pablo, the last being Finito, a short *torero* who was hit by the bull's horns each time he went in for the kill, exacerbating the tuberculosis that kills him. Says Pilar, "He was short of stature and he had a thin voice and much fear of the bulls. Never have I seen a man with more fear before the bullfight and never have I seen a man with less fear in the ring." Again, Finito is someone who displays enormous self-control, like Manuel Garcia and Pedro Romero—a goal Jake Barnes aspires to.

Pilar

Pilar is Hemingway's strongest, most developed woman character. "A woman about fifty ... almost as wide as she was tall ... and a brown face like a model for a granite monument." One thinks of Picasso's painting of Gertrude Stein. A sexual creature, she jokes she could take Maria from Jordan and him from Maria. But when she, Maria, and Robert visit the band of another Loyalist group in the mountains, they comfort Joaquín, a teenage boy, a failed bullfighter like Enrique of "Capital of the World," but one whose family has been killed. He tells them,

> When the fascists purified the town, they shot first the father. He had voted Socialist. Then they shot the mother. She had voted the same. It was the first time she had voted. After that, they shot the husband of one of the sisters. He was a member of the syndicate [union] of tramway drivers. Clearly, he could not drive a tram without belonging to the syndicate.... Then the husband of the other ... sister, who was also in the trams, had gone into the hills as I had. They thought she knew where he was. But she did not. So they shot her because she would not tell them where he was.

He begins crying, and Maria kisses him, saying we are all family now. Pilar states that if "Maria kisses thee again I will commence kissing thee myself.... Hold him, *Ingles*, till I get a good kiss at him." The boy replies, "'*Deja*,' the boy said and turned away sharply. Leave me alone." Pilar's reaction:

> "At times many things tire me," Pilar said angrily. "You understand? And one of them is to have forty-eight years. You hear me? Forty-eight years and an ugly face. And another is to see panic in the face of a failed bullfighter of Communist tendencies when I say, as a joke, I might kiss him."

Hilltop stand; crossed prayers

Another moving episode, one frequently excerpted, involves Sordo, the deaf one, and his band, including Joaquín, as they strive to steal horses so that all of Pablo's band can escape after the bridge is destroyed. They are noticed and chased, cornered on a small hill, "which had the shape of a chancre." They shoot their horses and fight behind them against the Nationalist forces downhill, Hemingway's version of Custer's last stand. Sordo thinks,

> living was a field of grain blowing in the wind on the side of a hill. Living was a hawk in the sky. Living was an earthen jug of water in the dust of threshing with the grain flailed out and the chaff blowing. Living was a horse between your legs and a carbine under one leg and a hill and a valley and a stream with trees along it and the far side of the valley and the hills beyond.

The writing is often poetic. Jordan's stream-of-consciousness musings are not; they are often long-winded, and the book would have benefited from their being edited.

Sordo and his small band are able to hold out for hours, although wounded, until planes come and bomb their position. Joaquin, though mortally wounded, still lives, and a Lieutenant Berrendo administers the *coup de grâce*, making the sign of the cross. Then Berrendo orders the heads of the members of the band cut off, both as proof of their demise and as a warning for other Republicans; he is a devout Catholic, but he also obeys his orders. He says five Our Fathers and five Hail Marys for the soul of a dead comrade, just as Joaquín had been saying the Hail Mary and the act of contrition as he was bombed. Later, riding back with the severed heads, Berrendo prays to "holy queen mother of mercy." He passes a hidden Anselmo keeping watch on the road, who prays to "Most kind, most sweet, most clement Virgin." There is bitter irony in both sides saying the same prayers to the kind and charitable Virgin Mary, even as they kill.

Cinematic cross-cutting

Pablo, on horseback, has seen the headless dead of Sordo's band. And that night, while Jordan sleeps, out of fear Pablo steals the exploder box and Jordan's detonators as a way to prevent the attack on the bridge, to save his life, that of his band, and the few horses he has accumulated through theft—peasant Pablo has aspirations to become a member of the middle class. Undeterred, Jordan continues. He will use grenades set off by wires through their pins to detonate the dynamite, although that means being closer to the blast. He also sends one of the band, Andrés, to the Loyalist commander of the attack with information Anselmo has gained watching the road, indicating that the Rebels are aware of the impending attack and have brought up reinforcements.

Throughout the novel, Hemingway included flashbacks of Jordan's visits to Gaylord's Hotel in Madrid and his interactions with the Communists there, military men, a journalist, Karkov, who is also an NKVD operative (Soviet secret service), and La Pasionaria, a woman propagandist for the Loyalists, based on Hemingway's own visits to Gaylord's. Jordan "liked to know how it really was; not how it was supposed to be. There was always lying in war." The scene at Gaylord's is brought in again later in the novel as the Communist Party officials and officers respond to the bridge and the subsequent attack, independent of Jordan.

Pablo, ashamed of his theft and feeling drastically and unbearably alone, like Judas after his betrayal of Jesus, returns with another band that was hidden in the mountains, so that they now have enough men to attack posts at either end of the bridge; Pablo will kill those of this second band who survive the attack, so that his band will have a sufficient number of horses to escape, to kill those who have just fought alongside him for the sake of his own band; tribal and political loyalty is extremely parochial. Intercut with the battle at the outposts and the placing of the hand grenades and dynamite at the bridge is Andrés' attempts to reach attack headquarters to warn of the mission's likely failure in the face of Rebel preparations. These chapters shorten as they go along, quickening the pace and heightening the suspense. Andrés encounters stupidity, bureaucratic inefficiency, and personal one-upmanship rather than cooperation toward a common goal. He contends with an anarchist commandant who would just as soon shoot him as take him to someone higher in command, then an orderly protecting his lieutenant colonel, in bed with his mistress, and so on. Finally, he is stopped by André Marty, political chief commissar of the International Brigades, an actual historical figure. Suspicious of anyone coming from behind the lines, of anyone not agreeing with him, Marty delays Andrés. A corporal under Marty says of him, "The old one kills more than the bubonic plague.... He kills rare things. Trotskyites. Divigationers. Any type of rare beast.... Always for political things." Finally, Jordan's message is delivered to the general in charge of the attack, too late to stop it; it comes just after Loyalist planes take off to bomb Rebel positions—positions that are now empty because the Rebels know the attack is coming.

Hemingway intrudes: "It is doubtful if the outcome of Andrés's mission would have been different if he ... had been allowed to proceed without Andre Marty's hindrance. There was no one at the front with sufficient authority to cancel the attack." Jordan, with hand grenades as blasting caps, detonates the dynamite and blows the bridge. Because of the need to be closer to the bridge without the detonator stolen by Pablo, Anselmo is killed by a piece of flying debris. Pablo's band escapes for a while, then confronts a small Fiat tank commanding a road they must cross. Coming at the end of the line and facing a now larger tank with a larger cannon, Jordan is injured when his horse, hit by shrapnel from a cannon blast, falls, and breaks Jordan's thigh, pinning him under. Knowing that he can't ride and determined to provide as much cover as he can for the fleeing band, Jordan says his goodbyes and has Pablo take tearful Maria from him and put her on a horse. They have lived full lives for three days. And as Jordan anticipates his soon-to-be death, he thinks, "I have fought for what I believe in for a year now. If we win here we will win everywhere. The world is a fine place and worth the fighting for and I hate very much to leave it."

Awaiting the Rebel troops that will pursue the Republican band, Jordan contemplates killing himself so he doesn't fall unconscious and be captured, then tortured to reveal what he knows. Earlier in the novel, when he had remembered his father's suicide, he called it an act of cowardice, and he rejects it now, despite the pain, and then adrenalin kicks in when he sees approaching Nationalist troops. The novel ends, as it began, with Jordan lying on his stomach on pine needles in the forest, now with his gunsights on approaching Lt. Berrendo.

Acclaim and a new life

The novel was an immense success: Scribners sold almost 300,000 copies, and the Book of the Month Club's cheaper edition sold nearly 400,000 more copies; in addition, Hemingway sold the movie rights for $136,000 (over $2.5 million today). The 1943 film starred Gary Cooper (too old for the role of Jordan) and Ingrid Bergman; though

Cooper and Bergman were nominated for awards, only Katina Paxinou won an Oscar, as best supporting actress for playing Pilar. The novel was unanimously nominated for the Pulitzer Prize of 1941 by the selection committee, but President Nicholas Murray Butler of Columbia, which administered the prize, vetoed their decision, calling the book offensive and profane; no prize for literature was awarded that year. But despite this national attention and praise, the leftists who expected a one-sided denunciation of fascism and an unadulterated praise of the Republican cause were disappointed and said so in print. They did not like the fact that Hemingway accurately portrayed the atrocities on both sides, the stupidities of war, as he had also done in *The Fifth Column*.

Pauline divorced Ernest in November 1940, with the agreement that he would pay $500 a month for Patrick and Gregory's support; while certainly fair overall, in light of Pauline's wealth and Ernest's widely fluctuating income—*Winner Take Nothing* made less than its $6000 advance in 1933—he considered it an attempt by her to annoy him. He married Martha later that month in Wyoming, and in December he purchased the Finca as a wedding present for her.

6. The War Years

Before 1940 was over, F. Scott Fitzgerald was dead of a heart attack at 44, Marty (Martha Gellhorn) had secured an assignment from *Collier's Magazine* to write on the war in China, and Ernest, securing a correspondent's role with a liberal journal PM, agreed to accompany her. They sailed from San Francisco to Hawaii, and from there to Hong Kong. Although Japanese troops were present, they stayed comfortably in a hotel with ample food and drink. In March 1941, they flew to Shaoguan, in Guangdong Province in southeast China, where the deprivations—mud, filth, lack of sanitary conditions, sickened Martha. She developed a fungus condition on her hands and feet and was repulsed by the Chinese army's snake wine: wine with small snakes coiled at the bottom, or bird wine, named for its bottled avian creatures. Hemingway, used to outhouses at Walloon Lake and no toilets when camping out, was not as disgusted as she, nor as repulsed by the food. In April, the couple flew to Chungking (now Chongqing) in south-central China, the war-time capital of the country besieged by Japanese forces who had attacked China in 1937. At Chungking, they met Generalissimo Chiang Kai-shek and Madame Chiang, who acted as translator; Hemingway also met secretly with Chou En-Lai, the Communist leader, whose intelligence impressed him: they might have been able to speak together in French since Chou En-Lai lived in Paris at the same time Hemingway had in the early 1920s. Ernest and Marty then flew along the Burma Road to Mandalay and Rangoon. She left to go to Jakarta, and he returned to Hong Kong and then back to the US. Both were interviewed in May 1941 by the Office of Naval Intelligence, and Ernest wrote a separate letter to the Secretary of the Treasury, Henry Morgenthau, advising US military aid to China; better to have the Japanese tied up fighting the Chinese than to be free to fight elsewhere. He also predicted that after the war with Japan, the Communists would continue to fight until they controlled China; his foresight turned out to be right. The couple returned to Cuba. Hemingway needed to stay out of the US six months of the year as a non-resident for tax purposes; his tax rate was over 70% of his income. But in September, the couple returned to Sun Valley. They left in early December for a trip to the Southwest, to the Grand Canyon, and on the way home, the news of the Japanese attack on Pearl Harbor reached them.

The Crook Factory, Sea Patrols, and *Men at War*

Hemingway offered his services to the North American News Alliance as a correspondent but was turned down: the war was going badly initially, and the Army did not want reporters at the front. Many Spaniards had come to Cuba after the Civil War, some veterans of Franco's forces, others with Fascist sympathies. Hemingway prevailed upon the US Ambassador to Cuba to allow him to set up an intelligence unit composed of ordinary Cubans who would listen for Axis sympathizers and keep an eye on them. Hemingway named this loose conglomerate of waiters, fishermen, jai alai players, prostitutes, and others, the Crook Factory. At the same time, he signed a contract with Crown Books to compile an anthology of war stories and worked on a long introduction. Meanwhile, German submarines were devastating US shipping on the East Coast and in the Caribbean, including shipments of oil from Texas and Louisiana to Europe, troop shipments, as well as armaments. So Hemingway decided to use the *Pilar* to scour the sea for German subs, persuading the ambassador to allow him to outfit the boat with a .50-caliber machine gun, a bazooka, and grenades to hurl down a sub's conning tower, should one surface near them in order to commandeer their fresh water and food. Marty denounced the adventure as a way to get rationed gasoline and go fishing every day. Ernest persisted throughout 1943, once seeing a sub but getting nowhere close to it, and never, through his own boat's effort or through the radio, managing to destroy a German sub.

His selection of stories for *Men at War* included the stories of David and Goliath and Joshua at Jericho, Virgil's account of the Trojan horse, the battle for Thermopylae in 34 BCE, Julius Caesar's account of the invasion of Britain, the Battle of Hastings in 1066, tales from the Crusades, those from the war against Napoleon as recounted by Stendhal and Leo Tolstoy, of the Civil War as told by Ambrose Bierce and Stephen Crane, the Russo-Japanese war of 1906—which the Japanese won; although his book was published during WWII, Hemingway admired brave men, whichever side they fought on. He included accounts of WWI, as told by Frederic Manning and T. E. Lawrence, the retreat from Caporetto from *A Farewell to Arms*, and Faulkner's story "Turnabout." Groups of stories were headed by quotations from German general and military tactician Carl von Clausewitz, and Hemingway concluded with a contemporaneous account of the battle of Midway in the Pacific. All were indicative of his wide reading. In his introduction, he said:

> The editor of this anthology, who took part and was wounded in the last war to end war, hates war and hates all politicians whose mismanagement, gullibility, cupidity, selfishness and ambition brought on the present war and made it inevitable. But once we have a war there is only one thing to do. It must be won.

And as for advice to young men going to war, Hemingway wrote that "I had a bad time until I figured it out that nothing could happen to me that had not happened to all men before me. Whatever I had to do men had always done. If they had done it, then I could do it too and the best thing was not to worry about it." Hence, this was a book of stories that told what men had done in war throughout recorded history. It was published, at nearly 1000 pages, in October 1942. The 1955 reissue dropped the Biblical accounts and Hemingway's short story of the Spanish Civil War, "The Chauffeurs of Madrid," that he had included in the original edition.

War: Domestic and International

Marty chastised him for his lack of cleanliness and increased drinking; during her absences, he drank heavily. Hadley had had no career and gladly stepped into the role of wife and helpmate; Pauline gave up her career at *Vogue* to become Hemingway's wife, caretaker, and editor. Martha had published eyewitness, first-hand accounts of the Depression, a novel, and a book of short stories before she met Hemingway. And after marrying him, she was determined not to give up her career. She continued to contribute journalism, and in 1943 completed a novel *Liana*. She then got a contract with *Collier's* covering the war for them and arrived in London in November. Bumby, Jack Hemingway, having left college and gone to Officers' Candidate School, was now overseas as a lieutenant with the Military Police. Hemingway was alone at the Finca with his cats, or on the *Pilar* with his sub-hunting crew. He sent Martha a cable, "Are you a war correspondent or wife in my bed?"

Although complaining of inaction, Ernest did nothing in the early months of 1944. Martha returned from England and said that Ernest belonged in Europe doing war coverage. In a dirty trick, he arranged with Collier's to be their European correspondent: US organizations could only have one accredited correspondent. That left Martha without official sanction or means of military transportation; she sailed back to Europe on a Norwegian cargo ship laden with dynamite. Hemingway flew to London in May—a month before D-Day. The British government arranged for him to fly with the Royal Air Force. In late May, coming home from a party in the early morning hours during a London blackout, Hemingway's inebriated driver drove into a water tower. In those days, before seat belts, he lurched forward, his head knocking the rearview mirror off its post and that post went into his forehead; his knees collided with the dashboard. He suffered another concussion, and it took 57 stitches to close his head wound. Martha, whose dynamite-laden ship had just arrived, was not sympathetic and scolded him for partying; meanwhile, he had met petite, busty blonde Mary Welsh, who was more sympathetic, although she was married at the time to Australian journalist Noel Monks and having an affair with novelist Irwin Shaw.

On June 5, he boarded a troop transport ship and later climbed down rope ladders on his swollen knees onto a landing craft. The army did not allow correspondents to land, so he observed from offshore of Omaha Beach; then it was back up the rope ladders and back to England. Marty, on the other hand, disguised herself as a nurse, walked onto a hospital ship, locked herself in the bathroom during the crossing, and went ashore with the stretcher-bearers. Ernest never forgave her for being at the scene of battle, while he was restricted to being a distant observer. Soon thereafter, she left England to cover the war in Italy, and Ernest returned to the RAF on a mission to bomb V-1 launching sites in France across the Channel, despite continuing headaches from his concussion; he also flew in a fighter that tried to shoot down the buzz bombs as they approached England. And with Marty gone, he intensified his pursuit of Mary Welsh.

In July, after a brief stint with George Patton's armored divisions, Hemingway turned up in the 22nd Regiment Headquarters of the 4th Infantry Division, headed by Col. Buck Lanham, as the division moved south through Normandy; Lanham would soon become a close friend. Ernest's French was an asset, as he could talk easily to the inhabitants of the area, gaining information. One day in early August, as he was coming back to Lanham's headquarters in the sidecar of a motorcycle, a German anti-tank gun fired on them. Ernest dove into a ditch and hit his head on a rock; it was his second concussion in three months, causing his headaches and double vision to return.

In the third week of August, Hemingway left the 22nd Regiment and headed east toward Paris. At Rambouillet, just 30 miles southwest of Paris, he met a group of Free French fighters armed mostly with recovered Luger pistols. He acted as liaison for them with the US Army. He also sought to obtain more substantial weapons for them. His irregulars (non-standard soldiers) went out, met other French, and gathered information about German locations, their tanks, antitank emplacements, and minefields. On August 25, 1944, Hemingway and his irregulars entered Paris, a day ahead of General Leclerc; General Eisenhower had given the privilege of taking Paris to Leclerc's troops. Hemingway claimed to have personally liberated the Traveller's Club and the Ritz Hotel, in which he immediately set up residence for himself and his irregulars. And he reunited with Mary Welsh, who flew from England with other reporters.

Military charges and two major battles

Meanwhile, Lanham and the 22nd had moved north and east into Belgium, as German forces retreated. Hemingway joined with them at the beginning of September, and they crossed the Rhine into Germany on the 12th. In early October, he was called back to France to face charges he had violated his obligations as a correspondent by taking up arms and commanding Free French forces at Ramboulliet; correspondents are supposed to be non-combatants. Hemingway perjured himself, saying he only acted as translator and intermediary between the French and the Army, and that the weapons he had obtained were in his room for storage only. He was acquitted, and later awarded a Bronze Star for his meritorious service as a war correspondent. He spent most of the rest of October in Paris with Mary. Jack Hemingway (formerly Bumby), who had joined the Office of Strategic Services, parachuted into France and was missing in action; he had been wounded and captured by the Germans and ultimately sent to a German prison camp commanded by an Austrian officer who had known him as a child in Schruns and who admired Ernest's fiction. Martha returned to Paris, learned of Mary, and asked for a divorce; the marriage was over, separated by distances and two ambitions. Martha also had begun a relationship with General James Gavin of the 82nd Airborne.

In mid-November, Hemingway rejoined Col. Lanham and the 22nd Regiment as they were ordered to clear a path through the Hürtgen Forest, the Hürtgenwald, which was protected by German artillery, mines, mortars, and machine guns, as well as a thick growth of trees and underbrush. In at least one attack by German troops, Hemingway responded to protect himself and those around him, including Lanham, with a Tommy gun he carried. In 18 days of combat, the regiment suffered 2,678 casualties—87 percent of its numbers. In early December, Hemingway returned to Paris with a severe cold.

On December 16, the Germans counterattacked with their Ardennes offensive, the Battle of the Bulge. Hemingway returned to the 22nd, still ill, but the German offensive was contained. At Christmas time, Martha returned to the Battle of the Bulge in Luxembourg, and through New Year's of 1945, Ernest and she continued to berate each other. He returned to Paris and Mary. Col. Buck Lanham arrived in Paris in February and gave Hemingway two German machine pistols. Hemingway used one to shoot at a picture of Mary's then-husband, Noel, which he had mounted on a toilet, shattering the toilet and flooding the bathroom. The repeated concussions, and his drinking, exacerbated his irrational impulse and rapidly shifting mood.

Home to the Finca and writing again

With a promise from Mary that she would follow, Ernest left Paris on March 6, 1945, and returned to Cuba, determined to restore the neglected house and return to writing. Mary arrived in early May, and Patrick and Gregory came down in June when school was out, followed by Jack, freed from a German prison, and needing to recuperate and fatten up. On June 20th, while driving Mary to the airport to see her parents, Hemingway's car skidded off the road and into a ditch. He cracked four ribs, his head against the rearview mirror, and his knees against the dashboard—again. Intermittent headaches kept bothering him all summer and fall. He restored his finances—he had only $499 in his checking account—with sales of movie rights of "The Killers" and "The Short Happy Life of Francis Macomber" for $112,500 ($1.635million today). And he began writing again in October.

He planned to write a Land, Sea, and Air book about the war, but quickly abandoned the Air part because of his limited time with the RAF, his lacking knowledge of the machines, the men, and their tactics. The Land part became first *The Garden of Eden*, with war elements incorporated into *Across the River and into the Trees*, and the *Sea* section broke into two parts: the larger one became *Islands in the Stream*; the other, *The Old Man and the Sea*—except for *Across the River* and *Old Man and the Sea*, they were published posthumously. Martha divorced him in late December, and he and Mary married in March 1946. By April, he had 700 pages of *Garden*, and 1000 by mid-July. It included Hemingway's hair fetishism, gender crossing, and sexual experiments with greater freedom than either publishing restrictions or his own reticence had previously allowed. But Hemingway was never able to finish this work to his satisfaction.

Mary discovered she was pregnant in July, and Ernest invited his sons to join him and Mary in Sun Valley. He and Mary drove from Florida, reaching Casper, Wyoming, on August 18th. Mary's pregnancy was ectopic; it ruptured her Fallopian tube, causing an internal hemorrhage, and she went into shock as her veins collapsed. The surgeon at the local hospital was on vacation, and the intern on duty could find no pulse and said there was nothing he could do. Hemingway told him to cut until he found a vein, into which Ernest inserted and manipulated a bottle of plasma. Mary's pulse resumed. Four more bottles of plasma, two transfusions, and time in an oxygen tent brought Mary gradually back to health. By

September, they were back in Sun Valley, together with the three boys, and in December they went to New York.

Back in Cuba in 1947, Ernest continued on his sprawling Garden of Eden manuscript. In April, Patrick was injured in a car accident while visiting Pauline in Key West. He came to Cuba with a headache, took his college board exams, but then turned violent and raving. Mary was absent, tending to her father in Chicago, who had prostate cancer. Pauline returned from Key West, and she and Ernest tended to Patrick for over a month. When Mary returned, she and Pauline became good friends. Patrick received electroshock therapy during July and August and recovered, but his illness after the concussion of the auto accident points to the family history of mental illness. Adding to what had been a terrible summer, Maxwell Perkins died in June. Hemingway went back to Sun Valley in September, hunting, fishing, and writing, and did not return to Cuba until February 1948. The spring and summer were spent fishing; he published nothing except an introduction to an illustrated *Farewell to Arms*. *Garden of Eden* was now a separate manuscript from what became *Islands in the Stream*. In September, the Hemingways sailed for Italy, and Ernest introduced Mary to Stresa and Cortina—places he had not seen in over 20 years—to Venice, and a return to a much-changed Fossalta, where he had been wounded in 1918. Duck hunting at Latisana in early December, Hemingway met and was immediately attracted to 18-year-old Italian Adriana Ivancich. He and Mary spent a quiet December and Christmas in Cortina. In January 1950, Mary broke her ankle skiing, and in February, Ernest got a terrible cold. Then, in March, he contracted erysipelas, a severe skin infection, most likely from dust on the roads which exacerbated a scratch near his left eye. Heavy doses of penicillin reduced the fever and the infection. Meanwhile, Malcolm Cowley's long "Portrait of Mister Papa" (Hemingway's nickname given to him by his sons, which he encouraged others to use, also) appeared in *Life* magazine, containing information, some accurate and some not, that Hemingway had given Cowley during a stay at the Finca the previous year. As Hemingway has said, all writers of fiction are liars, and with Cowley, as with others, he continued to exaggerate his exploits.

Hemingway set aside the Sea book—which became *Islands in the Stream*—and turned to writing a new book, located in Venice, with a protagonist for the first time his own age, dying of heart disease, in a relationship with a 19-year-old girl. The history of the protagonist, Col. Cantwell, would incorporate some of Hemingway's own wartime experiences, in Italy, in WWI, and in France in WWII, from his proposed Land book. At the end of April, the Hemingways sailed back to Cuba for more work on the book—interspersed with fishing. He got an offer from *Cosmopolitan* to serialize the new novel in its pages. The novel was not completed in November when the Hemingways left Cuba and stopped in NYC before sailing for France. In New York, Lillian Ross interviewed him for a *New Yorker* profile, and Hemingway, in ill-fitting clothes, for the most part, spoke pidgin English, except when discoursing about el Greco and Cézanne with her during a visit to the Metropolitan Museum of Art. It was an accurate reporting of how he looked and spoke—and Hemingway never blamed her—but the piece looked like a parody.

The Hemingway sailed back to Paris, then the south of France, where they celebrated Christmas in Provence, and Ernest took Mary to Le Grau du Roi, where he had honeymooned with Pauline. Then they drove on to Venice. In the past decade, Hemingway had only published *Men at War*, war dispatches for *Collier's*, several prefaces to his and others' books, and an article for *Holiday* magazine on the Gulf Stream as "The Great Blue River." He had survived another war, was 50, and was living largely from sales of his works to Hollywood—Twentieth Century Fox bought "My Old Man" for $45,00—but had published no fiction during the entire decade, except for one slight Spanish Civil War account in *Men at War*, "The Chauffeurs of Madrid," dropped at the second printing of that book.

7. Two Books, Two Plane Crashes

emingway continued his infatuation with Adriana Ivancich, writing her long letters and poetry from Cuba, inviting her and her mother to visit—Adriana's brother Gianfranco was already in Havana, a frequent guest of the Hemingways. *Cosmopolitan* began serializing *Across the River* in February 1950, a bowdlerized version of the novel. In July, while fishing on the *Pilar*, he slipped and opened his skull on a cleat—one more concussion. He wrote two brief children's fables for *Holiday*, one about a winged African lion, the son of the sculpture on St. Mark's Cathedral in Venice—a winged lion being a symbol both of St. Mark and of Venice. Hemingway's lion leaves Africa and flies to Venice, to Harry's bar, for a martini made with Gordon's gin and some Hindu trader sandwiches—not exactly a children's fable.

Across the River and Into the Trees

Across the River and Into the Trees was published by Scribners in September. It received poor reviews, and deservedly so: it is not a good novel. It recounts the final weekend of Colonel Richard Cantwell, stationed in Trieste after WWII, as he comes to Venice to see his 19-year-old girlfriend Renata (based on Adriana), shoot ducks, and die. The novel is dense with allusions, particularly to Dante—at one point, Cantwell says, "I am Mister Dante"—but also to Shakespeare, Eliot, Walt Whitman, François Villon, and others—showing how literate Cantwell is. It snipes at political figures, such as then-President Dwight Eisenhower as a politician/ general who never saw actual combat, and former President Harry

Truman and his daughter, as well as generals like Walter Bedell Smith and Bernard Montgomery. It also criticizes Cantwell's ex-wife, an ambitious journalist very much like Martha Gellhorn, but one nasty comment targets Mary, Hemingway's current wife, when he compares her blocked Fallopian tubes to the collapsed tubes of one of America's tire manufacturers. Cantwell is filled with spite. He also has a malformed right hand, shot through twice, a stigmata of sorts, that Renata treasures.

The novel opens with Cantwell being poled to a hunting blind by a surly boatman, suggestive of Greek mythology: Charon ferrying the dead to Hades. It then flashes back to before the trip to Venice, to when Cantwell passed a military physical exam by taking extra tablets of mannitol hexanitrate, a vasodilator, to combat his high blood pressure, to the buzzing he hears in his head and the nausea from the medication—the same experiences Hemingway had; Cantwell already has had three heart attacks, and his name suggests the physical activity he no longer can do well. He is then driven to Venice by T-5 Jackson, an uneducated soldier who relies on regulations in place of thought. Jackson's name links him to the source of the novel's title, Confederate General Stonewall Jackson, who said as he lay dying, "Let us cross over the river and rest under the shade of the trees," a quote Cantwell repeats at the end of the novel as he experiences his fourth and fatal heart attack. As they drive across the Venetian plain, Cantwell educates Jackson on the topography of the area and the history of his participation in WWI: he was an American lieutenant commanding Italian troops in the battles of the Corso, the Piave, and Mount Grappa, something most unlikely, especially considering his own admission of limited Italian at the time, but certainly enlarging upon and glorifying Hemingway's own stories of WWI service. It is a lecture Jackson finds boring.

We learn very little about Cantwell's life as a career military officer, where he served, or how he got from the Italian army into the American one. We learn he was an observer of the Spanish Civil War, but not actively engaged in it. Nothing of US military service prior to D-Day is disclosed. Cantwell was given charge of a regiment—Buck Lanham's 22nd Infantry—and status as a general for the battles of Hürtgenwald and the Battle of the Bulge, then demoted for losing most of his regiment in impossible terrain and against a well-placed, well-fortified enemy.

> Now every second man in it was dead and the others nearly all were wounded. In the belly, the head, the feet or the hands, the neck, the back, the lucky buttocks, the unfortunate chest, other places. Tree burst wounds hit men where they would never be wounded in open country. And all the wounded were wounded for life.
>
> "It was a good regiment," he said. "You might even say it was a beautiful regiment until I destroyed it under other people's orders."

Much of his bitterness toward the backroom generals is directed at their lack of front-line experience, their decisions based on maps alone. In a Dantesque manner, Cantwell assigns these theoretical generals and war profiteers to various circles of hell. And Renata, whose name means reborn, serves as the guide through his Purgatorio (purgatory), seeking to cleanse him of his bitterness, and to lead him to a peaceful death, which they both know is imminent.

There is a 30-year age gap between the colonel and Renata; she, as much as Maria in *For Whom the Bell Tolls*, is a sex object made up by Hemingway. A devout Catholic, she will not marry Cantwell because he is a divorced man—it is implied that he was married three times, but only the last ex-wife is excoriated. Not entirely devout, she explains that she cannot have sex with Cantwell because she is menstruating (no clear explanation; it is implied), so Cantwell sexually satisfies her manually three times under the blanket of a gondola in Venice's canals. Hemingway insisted that the Italian translation of the novel be delayed for two years to protect Adriana, but when it came out, there was a scandal nevertheless, with gossip—untrue—that she had been Hemingway's mistress. Years later, Adriana committed suicide.

Also based on Hemingway was Cantwell's excessive drinking. On the day he meets Renata in Venice, he has four martinis on an empty stomach, at least two of which are doubles, in addition to two gin and Camparis, and glasses of vermouth. At dinner, he shares a bottle of white wine with her, and at least one bottle of red wine, followed by several bottles of champagne, before their ride in a gondola.

After a day and a half with Renata, Cantwell joins his shooting companions, and early the next morning has his Charon take him to a duck blind, set in a river channel (the Tagliamento delta) that is frozen, so that few ducks descend within range. The next morning, he and Jackson drive back toward Trieste, and on the way there, Cantwell has his fatal heart attack. He has left instructions for Jackson to return a painting of Renata that she had given him to the Gritti Hotel where he had stayed; Jackson disobeys this final order; it will be returned, "through channels, Jackson thought, and put the car in gear." The work of art, like the novel, would now be left to the judgment of others.

Across the River is all thought and conversation. Besides the limited activity of breaking ice and duck hunting, the only action that occurs is when Cantwell beats up two sailors who whistled at Renata, an unlikely occurrence given that Cantwell breathes heavily simply climbing one of Venice's numerous bridges. It is also marred by some of Hemingway's peculiar constructions: Renata chewed "well and solidly"; Cantwell reached "accurately and well" for a bottle of champagne; while dying, Cantwell closed the car door "carefully and well." The repetition in these phrases, the addition of "well," may contribute to the rhythm of the sentences, but they add nothing to the meaning and they obtrude like pits in a fruit salad.

Hemingway said of the novel that he had "moved through arithmetic, through plane geometry and algebra, and now I am in calculus." Thus he intended much of the novel's meaning to be the implied, the seven-eighths of the iceberg below the surface. For example, Cantwell's numerous references to his dedication to his trade can be seen as Hemingway's self-reflexive comment about his own commitment to his craft, especially since Hemingway included phrases such as "in our time," "the sun rises," and that Cantwell "moved through different arms of the service as he had moved into and out of the arms of different women." But Renata remains a device, not a fully realized woman, and while her love may move Cantwell towards gentleness and forgiveness, that's not enough activity to sustain the novel for most readers. For those who were able to tie James Joyce's chapters in *Ulysses* to their corresponding episodes in *The Odyssey*, the hunt to connect each statement in *Across the River* to appropriate passages in Dante, Shakespeare, or Hemingway may be satisfying, but for most readers the novel is disappointing. And Hemingway was angry at the reviews.

Adriana, who had artistic pretensions, designed a cover for *Across the River*, which Scribners used to appease Hemingway, having them redone by a competent artist. Hemingway temporarily abandoned the *Islands in the Stream* portion of the Sea book and turned in early 1951 to the section that grew out of what he had outlined in his 1936 *Esquire* piece, about a Cuban fisherman catching and losing a giant marlin, and was well along by February. He then alternated on the two manuscripts, polishing *The Old Man and the Sea* and continuing *Islands*. Faulkner got the Nobel Prize instead of Hemingway, and in June Ernest's mother died. In September, after a summer of fishing and periodic work, Ernest received a call from Pauline from California. Gregory had been arrested for wearing women's clothes in a woman's restroom at a movie theater; he had been cross-dressing for years, and later would have sex-change surgery. Ernest and she argued. That night, September 30, 1951, Pauline, who had an undiscovered tumor on her adrenaline gland, causing extremely high blood pressure, burst a blood vessel and died in surgery. Ernest blamed Gregory, who blamed him back. They corresponded, met twice, but relations were never as cordial as they had been. However, Ernest was still paying Greg's medical school tuition up until his death.

The Old Man and the Sea

In January 1952, Charles Scribner III died, but as better news, *Life* magazine agreed to publish *The Old Man and the Sea* in a single issue, which it did in September. It sold 5,400,00 copies, followed by the Scribners edition of 133,650 copies, and that of Book of the Month Club, 153,000 books. On the three sales, Hemingway collected $136,588 ($1.348M, today). The book was dedicated to Max Perkins and Charlie Scribner.

The Old Man and the Sea is a novella in length, 118 pages in the paperback. It is not a novel, if a novel involves characters who grow and develop; Santiago, the protagonist of the book, does not change, although Manolin, Santiago's protégé and disciple, does assert his independence from his parents at the book's conclusion (Manolin is 22 years old.) The prose is a return to Hemingway's plain, less discursive style, more like the prose of *In Our Time* or *The Sun Also Rises*. Santiago, perhaps as a simpler man, has fewer interior monologues than either college instructor Robert Jordan or Colonel Richard Cantwell. The story can perhaps be best considered an extended beast fable. The story itself is simple: an old man, who hasn't caught a large fish for 84 days, day catches a large marlin on his 85th day; it tows him out to sea. He stays with the fish for two days and nights, and on the third day manages to kill it. But the fish is too large to be put into his small skiff, so he ties it alongside the boat and sets sail for home. And on the return night journey, sharks attack, stripping the marlin to its bones, despite Santiago's desperate efforts to preserve his prize. The old man returns the following morning only with a skeleton. But like *Across the River*, *The Old Man and the Sea* contains extended hidden strains of allusion and imagery.

In basic folklore terms, it is a night-sea journey of testing for the hero. The novella contains copious Christian imagery. Santiago (Spanish for St. James, a fisherman and patron saint of Spain) has line cuts in his hand—a stigmata—his back is scourged by the line across it as he seeks to take the weight from just his hands, and a crown of thorns of a sort: "the old man had been seeing black spots before his eyes and the sweat salted his eyes and salted the cut over his eyes and on his forehead." Most blatantly: "'Ay,' he said aloud. There is no translation for this word and perhaps it is just a noise such as a man might make involuntarily, feeling the nail go through his hands and into the wood." Hemingway is clearly making Santiago into a Christ figure, one whose suffering and endurance is a model for each of us, as one of the most quoted lines of the novella says: "A man can be destroyed but not defeated."

But Santiago is not alone in being likened to Christ: so is the marlin. As fish, it is ICTHYS, a Greek symbol of two intersecting arcs, as both the Greek word for fish and as an acrostic for Jesus Christ, Son of God, the Savior, the reason the early Christians drew the outline of a fish to identify themselves. Hemingway redoubles that identification when the fish rises from the depths on the third day, as Christ had risen from the dead on the third day, and when Santiago spears the fish in the side, as the Roman centurion speared Jesus on the cross.

Another major strain of imagery relates to baseball. The marlin's pointed bill is as long as a bat. Santiago reads the newspaper the night before he sets out and learns that Joe DiMaggio has broken out of his slump, hit three home runs, and led his team to victory, their 84th of the season. The game took place on Sunday, September 10, 1950; it was reported in papers on the 11th, and Santiago, who gets his papers a day late, reads it on Tuesday evening, September 12. DiMaggio is Santiago's hero, persevering despite a crippling bone spur, as Santiago must despite old age and bad luck. And, DiMaggio did lead his team that year to the pennant and a World Series triumph, despite his age; he retired the following year at 37.

The novel is set in 1950, during the Korean War. It includes a passage where Hemingway contrasts the handline fishers, such as Santiago, to those who use motorboats, set out buoys, and multiple lines with hooks—precursors of the longline fishing industry of today, which has depleted many fish stocks, especially that of sharks.

As in so many of Hemingway's works, Santiago wins the prize he seeks but cannot keep it. Nevertheless, he demonstrates courage, tenacity, and wisdom, despite the odds against him. Hemingway frequently said that, above all, one must endure—and get one's work done—and Santiago does both. Some critics saw the novella as an allegory: an aging Hemingway trying once more to gain a victory over the ravaging jaws of critics. But Hemingway, disingenuously, especially given his line about the sound a man might make as a nail is driven through his hand into wood, insisted that the sea was only a sea, the fish a fish, the old man an old man.

The novella was an immensely popular success, bringing huge quantities of fan mail, many visitors, and an offer by producer Leland Hayward to film it. It won the Pulitzer Prize for Literature in 1952. Meanwhile, Hemingway prepared for another African safari; much of the trip was underwritten by *Look* magazine, which sent along a photographer to illustrate text that Hemingway would contribute. In the spring of 1953, the Hemingways sailed for France and then drove to Spain, where Ernest had not been since 1938, and he was nervous about how he would be treated by the Franco government. He watched the Festival of San Fermines and the bullfights in Madrid, meeting young matador Antonio Ordóñez, the son of the bullfighter who had inspired Pedro Romero in *The Sun Also Rises*; Hemingway was greatly impressed by his bullfighting skills, became a friend, and would document Ordóñez's prowess in what became *The Dangerous Summer*.

Africa again, two plane crashes, and a prize

In August 1953, the Hemingways sailed through the Suez Canal to Mombasa, Kenya. From there, they went to the farm of Philip Percival, Ernest's guide, during his 1933-34 safari, at Kitanga. He shot fewer animals than he had 20 years before—still no elephants—and he also became an honorary game warden for the Kimana Region, responsible for killing animals that preyed on villagers' livestock. In addition to administering first aid and antibiotics, his official duties also included being on the lookout for possible Mau-Mau incursions during their revolt against British colonial rule that year. Hemingway also went native: he shaved his head, dyed his clothes to imitate Masai colors, hunted only with a spear alone at night, and professed to have a Wakamba bride named Debba. Mary was indulgent, saying he should claim his bride, but only after she had had a bath.

In late January 1954, as a belated Christmas present, Hemingway took Mary on a plane excursion over central Africa. They toured the Rift Escarpment, Lake Natron with its flamingos, the Ngorongoro Crater, and the Serengeti Plain. They stopped in Entebbe overnight, then on to the White Nile and Murchison Falls. Avoiding a flock of ibis, the pilot, Roy Marsh, descended and hit an abandoned telegraph wire, forcing a crash landing. Hemingway severely bruised his right shoulder, and Mary cracked two ribs. They spent an anxious night hoping not to be trampled by elephants coming to drink. They were rescued the next day by a boat that had been chartered by a British family, the same boat used a few years earlier in filming *The African Queen*, and taken to Butiaba, Uganda, on the shore of Lake Albert.

A plane had spotted and had seen their wreckage and seen no survivors. Hemingway was presumed dead. But at Butiaba the next day, a plane was ready to take them and Roy Marsh to Entebbe. The plane crashed on take-off and burst into flames. Marsh kicked out a window. He, Mary, and the pilot—sufficiently slim—left the plane that way. Ernest, too bulky, battered his way through the plane's jammed door. His sprained shoulder not allowing him to use it, he instead used his head as a battering ram, definitely gaining another concussion, and perhaps even breaking his skull. He received no thorough medical care or X-rays until months later in Venice. He complained of a collapsed lower intestine, broken vertebrae, damaged kidney, loss of vision in the left eye, and loss of hearing in the left ear. Some biographies report ruptured liver and spleen, but if these had occurred, he would have bled to death that day. Burns suffered from the plane fire were added to later when he tried to help put out a brush fire and, still unsteady on his feet, fell into it. The bodily injuries eventually healed; those to the head only exacerbated what had been accumulating for years and hastened his decline in the remaining seven years of his life.

In February, in Nairobi, he dictated, despite his physical condition, a 15,000-word article for *Look* to go with the pictures that had been taken. Like Santiago, he endured and got the job done. In late March, he and Mary reached Venice, where X-rays revealed he had a ruptured right kidney and two crushed vertebrae, and he finally received competent care for his burns. Those who met him then said he looked gray and diminished; minor efforts tired him, and movement hurt his back. He was driven to Spain and the bullfights in Madrid, and saw a doctor who told him to curtail his alcohol consumption; the Hemingways sailed back to Cuba in July.

During the summer, he wrote mainly letters, then turned to recording the recent African adventure, which became *True at First Light* and *Under Kilimanjaro*. In the fall, he was announced as the winner of the Nobel Prize for Literature. The prize is supposed to go to an inspiring book, and Hemingway's previous books were considered insufficiently uplifting; in fact, the prize citation called them "brutal, cynical, and callous." But Santiago's dedication and endurance were finally deemed inspiring; Hemingway's recent brush with death was likely also a contributing factor.

Hemingway declined to go to Sweden to receive the prize officially. The US ambassador to Sweden substituted for him, reading the speech Hemingway had written. It said, among other things:

> Writing, at best, is a lonely life.... For a true writer each book should be a new beginning where he tries for something that is beyond attainment. He should always try for something

that has never been done or others have tried and failed.... It is because we have had such great writers in the past that a writer is driven far out past where he can go, out where no one can help him.

That last line aligns him with Santiago.

8. Decline and Death

In 1955, Hemingway's back pain continued, and he was bothered by hordes of visitors coming to see the Nobel winner; even American college students came to Cuba and showed up at the Finca unannounced, interrupting his work on the African book. The only escapes were on the *Pilar* along the Cuban coast. Plans to film *Old Man and the Sea* continued, and some water scenes were shot outside Cojimar in August and September, but they didn't feature a giant marlin. Hemingway spent the end of the year and the beginning of 1956 in bed with symptoms of nephritis, hepatitis, and anemia. Nevertheless, pulp magazines in the 1950s regaled their mostly male readers with stories by and about Hemingway, the pinup for extreme masculinity. He was the most famous writer in the world.

In March, filming began in Cojimar with Spencer Tracy; Tracy's girth disturbed Hemingway, hardly that of a poor, near-starving Cuban fisherman. Hemingway put aside the African book and accompanied the film company to Peru in an attempt to catch a giant marlin on film. Although several were caught, including two by Hemingway, none weighed 1,000 pounds, and the fish ultimately used in the film is a man-made contraption of steel and rubber. Ernest was pleased that his back held up during the fishing but was unhappy with the time taken from his writing. He returned to the Finca and wrote several unpolished short stories based on his experiences in WWII, and two very bad ones, with loss of sight a theme in each. In September, he and Mary sailed from New York to Paris, and from there they drove to Spain for the summer bullfighting season. Hemingway had arranged for another trip to Africa, but that plan was derailed when the Suez Crisis of 1956 closed the Canal. He and Mary spent the winter in Paris, Ernest dieting and trying to lower his cholesterol. He joined Archie MacLeish and poet Robert Frost by mail to get Ezra Pound released from St. Elizabeth's Hospital, where he had been imprisoned after being found guilty of treason and declared insane for broadcasting to US troops during the war. Frost, as the least politically toxic of the group, went to Washington the following year and got Pound released, at which point he returned to Italy in his daughter's care; Hemingway had a large FBI file on him ever since his days supporting the Spanish Republic during their civil war and during his Crook Factory days in Cuba, when FBI agent Raymond Leddy regularly reported on him to J. Edgar Hoover.

Back at the Finca in spring 1957, when he was asked by the *Atlantic* to contribute to their centenary edition, Hemingway began a memoir of F. Scott Fitzgerald that later would go into *A Moveable Feast*. Instead of that remembrance, he gave the *Atlantic* his two short stories about blindness. They were published in November of that year and were the last pieces of fiction published in Hemingway's lifetime; they added no luster to his reputation. While not fishing, he worked on the Paris book, sketches of his acquaintances during his early years in the city and those he knew then, alternating that work by returning to and expanding *The Garden of Eden*, bringing it to 48 chapters and over 200,000 words. To the *Garden* manuscript, he added material based on his recent safari, the African story of that published book. The domestic scene alternated between successful days of writing and fishing and loud arguments with Mary; she told him, and others, that she would leave him because of his drinking and abusive ways, go to New York City and restart her journalism career—but she never did.

In the fall of 1958, Ernest and Mary drove to a rented house in Ketchum, Idaho, and went bird hunting: ducks, pheasants, and quail. The movie version of *the Old Man and the Sea* came out in October to generally bad reviews, although it won an Oscar for its musical score. Hemingway ignored it; the film had taken too much of his precious time. In January 1959, dictator Fulgencio Batista fled Cuba for Santo Domingo, and Fidel Castro took control of the country. Hemingway worked on both the Paris sketches and *Garden*. In March, he bought the house in Ketchum that would be his last residence—and the site of his suicide—and he returned to Cuba on Easter Sunday. He planned to go back to Spain for the summer of bullfighting, for *mano a mano* contests between Antonio Ordóñez and his brother-in-law Luis Miguel Dominguín; two of Dominguín's brothers were managers of both bullfighters and, no doubt, arranged the joint contest to attract more ticket-buying spectators. Hemingway's account of these bullfights became the basis for a *Life* magazine article and a book, *The Dangerous Summer*.

A dangerous summer

The Hemingways were hosted by Bill Davis and his wife at their home, La Consula, near Malaga, Spain; Davis also drove Ernest around the country for most of the *ferias*. At the end of May, a bull gored Ordóñez in the buttocks but Ordóñez killed him nevertheless, and he accompanied Hemingway to Malaga to recuperate. Throughout June and early July, Hemingway, with Davis at the wheel, crisscrossed Spain, attending bullfights and getting little sleep. Mary spent a month preparing an elaborate 60th birthday party for Ernest at La Consula, despite having broken her toe recently. Among those present were Gianfranco Ivancich and his wife, Buck Lanham and his wife, Ordóñez and his wife—whose birthday coincided with Ernest's—A.E. Hotchner—who had secured the serialization of *Across the River* for *Cosmopolitan* and had lately been adapting Hemingway's short stories for television—and Valerie Danby-Smith, a 19-year-old Irish journalist who had tried to interview Hemingway in Pamplona and was now his latest teenage crush. The party was largely a success. Ernest shot cigarettes out of Ordóñez's mouth with an air gun. But Ernest was openly and obscenely abusive toward Mary and, at one point, berated Buck Lanham, dampening their friendship. His mood swings became more violent, as his father's had been.

In August, Dominguín was gored in the groin, and three days later,

Ordóñez was also gored. Later in the month, despite their wounds, the two fought the bulls once more, and Dominguín received another horn wound, and in a separate fight, Ordóñez sustained a foot wound (the bull trampled him). As Hemingway returned to La Consula, a front tire blew out, the car went off the road, and the front end was demolished. That was enough of witnessing bullfighting for him. He stayed at La Consula until early October, working on his account of the *mano a mano* contest for *Life*. The magazine had only wanted some 10,000-word captions for photos taken by a staff photographer, but Hemingway turned his copious notes into a full-length book.

Ernest sailed back in late October; Mary had already flown to get the Finca ready. In New York, Hemingway delivered to Scribners his Paris sketches, saying that he needed to go over them once again before they were published. He had great difficulty with the ending, his separation from Hadley: he did not want to blame Pauline, and he did not want to take any personal responsibility. The exact wording to solve those problems eluded him. He and Mary returned to Ketchum in November, and, while out hunting with Ernest, Mary slipped and fractured her elbow. Ernest groused that running to the hospital interrupted his work on the *Life* article and the Paris sketches. In January, they returned to Cuba and the Finca, and Valerie Danby-Smith was invited to join them as Ernest's secretary. By May, he had nearly 120,000 words, 688 typed pages on the Ordóñez-Dominguín contests, which was a problem, since *Life* had wanted only 10,000 words. Hemingway had 12 times that and he couldn't edit the manuscript; in addition, his eyes were bothering him and he was not sleeping well. He invited A. E. Hotchner to help him cut the bullfighting manuscript's bloated size. They reduced it by over half, and *Life* paid $90,000 for what they released in three consecutive issues on September 5, 12, and 19, 1960; Hemingway's originally submitted manuscript was published by Scribners in 1985 as *The Dangerous Summer*. Throughout all versions, Hemingway had shown marked favoritism for Ordóñez over Dominguín. But before finally releasing the manuscript, Hemingway said he had to go back to Spain for that season's bullfights, and more particularly, that Ordoñez needed him because they were a team. These delusions of grandeur were repeated when he told Hotchner to demand $900,000 from Twentieth-Century Fox for *The World of Nick Adams*, a film based on Hotchner's TV adaptations of the short stories; the film was eventually released as *Hemingway's Adventures of a Young Man* in 1962, with a screenplay by Hotchner, and Hemingway received $125,000 from the studio for rights to film the stories. Hotchner felt Hemingway had shrunk: his massive chest and shoulders were no longer there.

To the Mayo and back

From Spain, Hemingway wrote Mary that he feared "a complete physical and nervous crack up from deadly overwork." He believed that Bill Davis was trying to kill him, and his kidneys were bothering him again. Physically and mentally, he was deteriorating. He flew back to New York and Mary in October, and they took the train, rather than Ernest's usual way of crossing the country by driving, back to Ketchum. He believed the FBI was after him, monitoring his bank accounts; the FBI kept tabs on him, but not to the extent Hemingway's paranoia imagined. He was also worried that he might be in trouble with immigration authorities over Valerie Danby-Smith's status in the country. It was clear to Mary and his local doctor, George Saviers, that he needed treatment. With the stigma against mental illness very much present in the country, Mary and Saviers had him enter the Mayo Clinic in Rochester, Minnesota, for high blood pressure; Saviers had recorded readings of 250/125, despite the medication reserpine that Hemingway was taking to control his hypertension. To prevent the press from finding out, Hemingway was signed in as George Saviers on November 30, 1960, and he was placed in the care of Dr. Hugh Butt, physician, and Dr. Harold Rome, psychiatrist. On admission, he weighed 175 pounds, far below the over 200 pounds he normally carried. He was found to be mildly diabetic—as his father had been—with an enlarged liver, probably caused by alcoholism. His blood pressure was 220/150, but the doctors blamed his depression on the reserpine he had been taking and switched medications. After these preliminary examinations, Dr. Rome prescribed electroconvulsive (electroshock) therapy for his depression, and Hemingway received two treatments a week through the rest of December and early January. The treatments temporarily destroyed his memory and ability to speak, but he and Mary joined the Butt family for Christmas dinner, where they sang songs in Spanish, French, and German. At another dinner in January, Dr. Butt allowed small amounts of wine; Ernest also went shooting with Dr. Butt and his son and demolished 27 clay pigeons in a row and wine bottles with a .22 pistol at 110 feet. His memory affected, but the eye and hand coordination remained intact. Meanwhile, word of his hospitalization "for hypertension" at Mayo leaked. He was invited to the John F. Kennedy inauguration but declined because of health, and he talked his doctors into believing that writing was his best cure; he was discharged on January 22, 1961. They believed the electroshock therapy would cure his depression; it did not. They never considered his multiple concussions or what his alcoholism might have done to his brain. Ernest said at the time, "[W]hat is the sense of ruining my head and erasing my memory, which is my capital, and putting me out of business? It was a brilliant cure but we lost the patient." His reason for living had been his writing, and now he couldn't write. Moreover, he told a Ketchum friend that he feared when next hospitalized he would be institutionalized for life.

Hemingway was flown back in a small plane. He worked trying to arrange to his satisfaction the order of the Paris sketches and to write an introduction. In February, he was asked to contribute to a volume of congratulations to newly elected President Kennedy, and he struggled for hours trying to string sentences together. They wouldn't come. Even his letter-writing diminished in volume, along with his weight: he was now down to 164 pounds; also, he now combed hair from the back, forward, over his bald head. And despite the shock therapy, his paranoia returned: he was broke, the FBI had bugged his house and car, immigration authorities were after him, Mary just wanted his money. The Bay of Pigs invasion occurred on April 15; Ernest knew now that Cuban-American relations were completely sundered and that he would never return to the Finca, his boat, his library there, his friends, and his large cache of manuscripts, including what would become *Garden of Eden* and *Islands in the Stream*. His suicidal thoughts increased. He wrote Charles Scribner, Jr., telling him not to publish the Paris book yet; he didn't have a title, he still was having difficulties with the conclusion, and he was afraid of libel suits. This last was another sign of his paranoia: he was particularly concerned about Ethel Moorhead, publisher of *This Quarter*, a journal he had contributed to in the 1920s; Moorhead had been dead since 1955.

After the Bay of Pigs, on April 21, Mary found him in the kitchen of their Idaho home holding a shotgun. She talked desperately to him until Dr. Saviers came by to do his daily blood pressure check. Dr. Saviers took the gun from Hemingway, had him admitted to Sun Valley hospital under heavy sedation, and he and Mary arranged for readmission to the Mayo Clinic. On the car ride to the airport, they stopped at home so that Ernest could pick up some clothes. He immediately grabbed a shotgun and loaded it before he could be stopped. Back to the Sun Valley Hospital, and two days later, he was on a small plane to the Mayo. At a stop, he got out to stretch his legs and tried to walk into the propellors of a taxiing plane.

At the Mayo, electroshocks resumed. And again, Ernest convinced his psychiatrist that work was the best cure for him, that he needed to get back to writing—except that he couldn't. He was discharged on June 26, and his psychiatrist's notes have never been made public. A friend drove them back, and it took five days to cover the 1700 miles between Rochester and Ketchum, arriving on June 30. July 1 was a quiet day spent seeing friends and dining at a local restaurant. The next morning, Ernest found the keys to the locked gun cases in the basement, took out a double-barreled gun and loaded it, went up to the foyer of the house, and, holding the gun's butt to the floor and its barrels to his forehead, tripped both triggers. He was 61, three weeks short of his 62nd birthday, and a week short of the 43rd anniversary of his wounding in Italy. His life was over, but new books would continue to appear.

9. The Posthumous Works

A Moveable Feast

The first posthumous publication was the Paris sketches, published as A *Moveable Feast* (1964). Although Hemingway mocked Fitzgerald for the latter's notoriously poor spelling, Hemingway himself often did not consult a dictionary—no spellchecker, no computers then; "moveable" is his own spelling, and Scribners kept it. The manuscript as Hemingway had submitted it to Scribners in 1959, was largely complete. Mary edited with Harry Brague, a Scribners editor. She shifted chapters and changed Hemingway's insistence in the preface that the work was one of fiction. It is so, of course: any remembrance of things past is shaped by time and memory; it is shaped by the author for maximum effect; and Hemingway may have wanted a fiction label to avoid suits of libel. Mary also supplied the title; Hemingway could not find a satisfactory one, although he seriously considered "The Eye and the Ear" from Ecclesiastes, shortly after the passages where the sun rises. The title of the book came from a 1950 letter Ernest had written Hotchner in which he had said that "If you are lucky enough to have lived in Paris as a young man, then wherever you go for the rest of your life, it stays with you, for Paris is a moveable feast."

Moveable Feast is a bitchy book, full of nasty sniping about onetime friends and benefactors: Stein, Fitzgerald, Ford Madox Ford, Gerald Murphy, and John Dos Passos. As someone said of Hemingway, he was always willing to lend a hand to someone higher up on the ladder of success than he was. (Not entirely true, he could often be, and was, very generous to those needing help. Complexity again.) The only friends from Paris who come off well are Sylvia Beach, poet Evan Shipman, and Ezra Pound. The chapter on Ford and the Devil's Disciple came from *The Sun Also Rises*, from which it had been cut. The book portrays Hemingway as a starving artist, right out of *La Bohème*, ignoring the money that supported them from Hadley's trust fund. Hadley is constantly portrayed as loving, supportive, and acquiescent. And perhaps she was. Pauline, who is never mentioned by name, is described as "an unmarried young woman [who] becomes the temporary best friend of another young woman who is married, goes to live with the husband and wife and then unknowingly, innocently and unrelentingly sets out to marry the husband." If she unrelentingly determines to marry the other woman's husband, then her actions are neither unknowing nor innocent. And Hemingway portrays himself as much the victim of her predation as Hadley.

Ford is depicted as a pompous, wheezing ass. (His wheezing came from being gassed in WWI, for which he enlisted at the age of 41.) Stein, though helpful, is too lazy to revise her work and is primarily interested in herself. She will not praise any authors who have not praised her. And she instructs Hemingway that female homosexuality is fine and beautiful, while male homosexuality is ugly and repugnant, sick. The break between them, as Hemingway depicts it, comes when Hemingway hears the desperate pleadings of Stein to her domineering lover, Alice Toklas, and implies his embarrassment at returning.

Fitzgerald is a drunk who can't hold his liquor, is late for appointments, and worse, he's controlled by his wife, something Hemingway had seen in his parents' marriage and had determined never to allow in his. The two go together to retrieve a car whose top Zelda had cut off, and then abandoned in the rain, and Fitzgerald also reveals himself to be a hypochondriac. Worse yet, Hemingway wrote that Fitzgerald's "talent was as natural as the pattern that was made by the dust on a butterfly's wings. At one time he understood it no more than the butterfly did and he did not know when it was brushed or marred"—implying that Scott was a thoughtless author, employing "natural talent," and not thought, planning, careful revision. Yet Hemingway followed Fitzgerald's advice in pruning the opening of *The Sun Also Rises*, and Fitzgerald's criticisms of *A*

Farewell to Arms, which Hemingway ignored, are quite cogent. Worst of all, Scott doubts his masculinity, saying that his penis is too small to satisfy Zelda, and turns to Hemingway for reassurance. Ernest examines him in a restroom, then takes him to the Louvre to examine the phalluses on Greek statuary, and finally gives advice on sexual matters—playing Papa to someone three years his senior. And Zelda, Hemingway declares, is insane.

Moveable Feast—The Restored Edition

Seán Hemingway, Gregory's son and Ernest's grandson, and Patrick Hemingway, Ernest's second son, have begun a cottage industry of reissuing Hemingway's books with introductory material by each of them, and additional items—pages of manuscript, deleted portions—largely culled from the Hemingway collection at the John F. Kennedy Library. These reissues, under the collective title of the Hemingway Library Edition, do not change any of the subsequent publications, books Hemingway himself saw into print. But Seán's and Patrick's edition of *A Moveable Feast*, called by them "The Restored Edition" (2009), was an attempt to restore the image of Pauline, Patrick's mother, and Seán's grandmother. Nevertheless, it includes the passage where unnamed Pauline "unrelentingly sets out to marry the husband" of her friend. The Restored Edition also includes a section where Ernest, unlike the first published edition, takes blame himself: "I have never tried to apportion the blame, except my own part, and that was clearer all my life.... Any blame ... was mine to take and possess and understand." So, some of the onus is off Pauline.

Hemingway also, in his drafts, tried to establish an extended metaphor linking skiing to writing. In those early days, before ski lifts, he says, one had to climb the mountain before one could ski it down, one had to develop the requisite muscles. Hemingway tries to link it to his learning of his craft as he rewrites *The Sun Also*

Rises. He could never get the metaphor to his satisfaction, and Mary reduces it in the original volume to "[W]e built the ability to do it and have it with the long climbs carrying heavy rucksacks. We could not buy the trip up nor take a ticket to the top. It was the end we worked for all winter, and all winter built to make it possible." The Restored Edition has several paragraphs about skiing over different pages, but no clearer expression of the metaphor. It is worth noting that Hemingway at Schruns was doing Alpine skiing on a leg and knee operated on seven years before. There is a picture of him with Pauline at the beach at San Sebastian in 1927, and he is wearing an elastic brace on that operated right knee. He may have continued skiing at Sun Valley; I can find no confirmation of this. In addition to his fishing—hauling in fish weighing hundreds of pounds—he played tennis and swam regularly at the Finca, even while bits of shrapnel continued to work their way out of his legs in the 1930s.

Mary's editing of the original edition surrounds the three chapters on Scott Fitzgerald with memories of Paris days, with, in conclusion, a long chapter on skiing in Schruns, the insertion into their lives of John Dos Passos, the Murphys, and Pauline, all unnamed, with Schruns abandoned by them; Paris and the Hemingways' marriage unalterably changed. The Restored Edition's main text ends with the size of Fitzgerald's penis, an ignominious ending indeed, with the original ending appended in "Additional Paris Ketches," along with two chapters that Mary had included in her edited text. Seán Hemingway adds two more chapters about Fitzgerald. One dates from 1928 in Baltimore and thus is plainly unlike the life around Paris. The other astounding chapter features three-year-old Bumby commenting on the attractiveness of passing prostitutes and ordering a small beer as an exemplary model for frequently drunk Fitzgerald. There is one poignant addition Seán includes, a fragment Ernest wrote in April 1961, some two months before his suicide, and after his first round of shock therapy at the Mayo, attempting once again to pen a satisfactory conclusion. It ends: "[T]his book contains material from the *remises* [storage places] of my memory and of my heart. Even if one has been tampered with and the other does not exist." That his heart does not exist is a clear forewarning of the suicide to come.

Islands in the Stream

The next posthumous book was *Islands in the Stream* (1970), a pared-down version of Hemingway's sprawling Sea Book. He had wrestled with the book for years, alternating between two possible protagonists, painter Thomas Hudson and writer Roger Davis. There is, thus, the concern with creativity, with expression, the art of both men, as he had wrestled with the skiing metaphor for art in *Moveable Feast*, a theme that will occur again in *Garden of Eden*. Hudson, a realistic painter in the style of Winslow Homer, is named for an explorer and another blue stream, like Santiago's Gulf Stream. Both Hudson and Davis had lived in Paris in the 20s, and Hudson's reminiscences, being Hemingway's, are more of writers than of painters. The final part of the manuscript Hemingway separated and published as *The Old Man and the Sea*, presumably a work of fiction by Roger Davis. Another long fragment was published in the Finca Vigia edition of the short stories as "The Strange Country," in which Davis has just returned from writing a movie in Hollywood as the Spanish Civil War unfolds. In this variant, he is the father of the sons that, in *Islands*, are Hudson's children; he also, like Hemingway, had a former wife who lost his manuscripts while bringing them to him; in short, he's a version of the author, as is Hudson, and in this version, Roger Davis is making love to a compliant, beautiful 22-year-old, whom he calls "daughter."

The published book is divided into three parts: Bimini, Cuba, and At Sea. Hudson, who has inherited oil money and a ranch in Montana, lives most of the year in Bimini, the westernmost island in the Bahamas, where Hemingway often fished. Hudson's house, the opening lines declare, "was built on the highest part of the land between the harbor and the open sea. It had lasted through three hurricanes and it was built solid as a ship." Hudson's three sons visit him during their summer breaks. Tom is the eldest, named after his father, Davy the middle son, and Andy, the youngest. They are patterned after Ernest's three sons, Jack, Patrick, and Gregory. Young Andy "was born being very old. He was a devil, too ... and he had a dark side to him that nobody except Thomas Hudson could ever understand. Neither of them thought about this except that they recognized it in each other and knew it was bad and the man respected it and understood the boy's having it." Is this a reference to depression, from which both Ernest and Gregory suffered? Or is it a coded reference to Gregory's transvestism and eventual gender-switching "that they recognized ... in each other"; then it also is an admission by Hemingway of his own feminine impulses.

There are two exciting episodes in "Bimini," both involving middle son Davy. In the first, he is spearfishing, and the blood attracts a hammerhead shark. As Davy desperately swims back to the safety of their boat, Hudson tries to kill the fast-approaching shark with a rifle but misses repeatedly. The alcoholic mate shoots the shark with Hudson's Tommy gun, saving Davy. In the second episode, Davy, thirteen years old, fights for six hours to land a swordfish, only to lose it. The fight is too close in content and outcome to Santiago's in *The Old Man and the Sea*, which may have strengthened Hemingway's impetus to remove OMS from the Sea book and publish it separately. The parallels between the two texts are close. Davy says of the fish, "I love him more than anything on earth," as Santiago calls the fish his brother and says, "Fish, ... I love you and respect you...." Davy's hands bloody, his feet battered, his back scourged by the fishing harness, learns that human efforts are sometimes not enough, but like Santiago, he endeavors and endures. David and Andy return to their mother in France, and all three are killed in an auto wreck, probably suggested by the accident Patrick and Gregory Hemingway were in while visiting Pauline in 1947. Roger Davis, who in both episodes is close and supportive to the boys while Hudson runs the boat, disappears at the end, not to surface in the next two parts.

The second section of the book, "Cuba," is the weakest. It moves forward to WWII, and Hudson has remarried a woman correspondent, much like Martha, who is away and writes to him. He goes to sea sub-chasing, as Ernest did, and he has long, windy conversations with his cat and with patrons at Havana's Floridita bar. He has a brief, sexual re-encounter with his first wife, a movie actress. Finally, he gets word that his remaining son, his namesake Tom, a flyer, has been shot down and killed over France. He is now alone. And he stops painting—of which we have very few technical details; Hemingway no more convinces me that Hudson is a painter than he convinced me that Frederick Henry was a student of architecture.

The final section, "At Sea," involves Hudson and his crew pursuing a damaged German U-boat. The sub lands, its crew disembarks, murdering civilians and stealing boats as it moves along the Cuban coast, supplying themselves, looking to be rescued, and staying just ahead of Hudson and his boat and crew, the members of which are barely individualized, too little to become characters in their own rights. Standing on the bridge of his boat, in a narrow channel, Hudson is shot three times. His crew kills the Nazis, but the novel ends with Hudson dying.

The novel adds nothing to Hemingway's stature. The episodes with Davy in "Bimini" and "The Sea Chase" might have been published as separate long short stories; the talkative "Cuba" detracts from the entirety, showing, as "The Dangerous Summer" did, his inability to edit his verboseness or to shape a coherent tale in his final years.

The Nick Adams Stories

In 1972, Scribners published The Nick Adams Stories, a compilation of the stories in which Nick appears, and two in which he may be, but isn't named ("The Light of the World" and "In Another Country"), selected by academician and critic Philip Young and arranged by him in what he thought was their chronological order. It was an attempt to create Nick as a cohesive character—even though he's shot in the spine in one story and then hikes and skis in stories following—and the stories as a cumulative biography of a central figure in Hemingway's oeuvre. In addition to the previously published stories, Young included parts cut by Hemingway before publication from "Indian Camp" and "Big Two-Hearted River," as well as unpublished fragments and stories. In the "Indian Camp" excerpt, we see young Nick's cowardice as he fires a rifle to call his father back to camp; in what had been intended as a conclusion to "Big Two-Hearted River," Nick discourses on writing in a garrulous fashion, unlike his closed-mouthedness in the story proper. The fragments of what might be begun novels and a sketch about Northern Michigan's Ojibwe don't add much to what we already know. The only major addition is an unpublished story called "The Last Good Country," where Nick escapes from game wardens for killing a deer out of season and hides in the virgin forest with sister Littless in a near-incestuous adventure. It is based on Hemingway's own scrape with game laws for killing a heron, but, while developing interesting characters, has no resolution.

The Dangerous Summer

In 1985, as mentioned above, Scribners published Hemingway's 1959 manuscript about the *mano a mano* contests between Ordóñez and Domenguín, without the editing done by Hotchner and *Life* magazine. This edition featured a 37-page introduction by James Michener, who only met Hemingway once and may have been chosen by Scribners for this task because of his lengthy travel book, *Iberia*. Scribners included in Mitchener's intro his glossary on Spanish bullfight terms, redundant because they also included Hemingway's glossary from *Death in the Afternoon*. On the other hand, they eliminated from Hemingway's text the names of other bullfighters and the descriptions of their fights, keeping only the accounts of Ordóñez and Dominguín, and maintaining the book's focus strictly on the *mano a mano* contest.

Much of Hemingway's garrulousness has been pruned, but his egotistical attitude has not: he is important for morale and for an accurate assessment of the bullfight. He assumes that the bull is killed in a certain manner "to please me." Sentences that appear in *Life* have been silently edited: a dangling modifier corrected, "safer than" changed to "as safe as." Yet the descriptions of the actual encounters with the bulls hold their magic, as do others, such as this one:

> [We saw] where two storks were nesting on the roof of a house.... The nest was half built, the female had not laid her eggs yet and they were courting. The male would stroke her neck with his bill and she would look up at him with storklike devotion and then look away and he would stroke her again.

Again, as with painter Hudson and writer Davis, Hemingway turns to a discussion of art, as he had in *Death in the Afternoon*:

> A bullfighter can never see the work of art that he is making. He has no chance to correct it as a painter or writer has. He cannot hear it as a musician can. He can only feel it and hear the crowd's reaction to it. When he feels it and knows that it is great it takes hold of him so that nothing else in the world matters.

As a recent book on Hemingway is aptly titled, for him "art matters": the capture of the instant, the representative facts that captured motion and signified emotion, the leaving out what was inessential and could be supplied by a knowledgeable reader, the subtle allusions, and the repetitions and rhythms, the alliteration and assonance. It was there at the beginning, and parts of it remained, despite the depression, the concussions, the alcoholism, and the multiple medications and supplements he took.

The Garden of Eden

The Garden of Eden pared down from Hemingway's 1500 manuscript pages to a 247-page book, is the creation of Hemingway and Tom Jenks, the editor whom Scribners hired. Jenks cut two-thirds of the manuscript—which Hemingway could not control after fifteen years of intermittent tinkering—and left out three major characters whose lives and desires reflect on those of the remaining characters, newlywed David and Catherine Bourne, and Marita. Omitted are painter Nick Sheldon and his wife Barbara and their writer friend Andy Murray. Also omitted are references to works of art that influence the characters. In the manuscript, the Bournes and Sheldons visit the Rodin Museum in Paris and observe the *Metamorphosis of Ovid*, a study Rodin made for his *Gates of Hell*. The statue figures two nude women embracing, one kneeling, the other recumbent. On *The Gates of Hell* they are identified as "The Damned Women," and Rodin included it as an indicator of the lesbianism then in Paris. Barbara conceives a passion for Catherine that is never consummated, but she does sleep with Andy on the same day that Nick, her husband, is killed in a bicycle accident; in guilt and remorse, Barbara commits suicide. Catherine, however, does have an affair with Marita.

The other artwork omitted is Bosch's *The Garden of Earthly Delights*, a triptych, with the left-hand panel showing a chaste Edenic scene and the right-hand panel depicting hellish torments, including males being sodomized, and the central panel showing both heterosexual and homosexual pairings. This garden would seem to be subsumed in the novel's title, but Jenks also cut all references to it; only a mention of Catherine's visiting the Prado in Madrid, home of the painting, survives.

The published novel opens on David and Catherine's honeymoon at Grau du Roi, where Hemingway and Pauline honeymooned and covers some seven months in 1923. Catherine is rich, as Pauline was; David is in his mid to late twenties, an American who was raised in Africa, and a WWI veteran, a former flyer. He is the author of two novels, the most recent about the war, and reviews have come as his novel has gone into a second printing. Catherine is jealous of the clippings, later accusing David of committing onanism with them. She is a failed artist, unable to bring forth a child, or a written, painted, or sculpted work, and that lack of artistic expression besets her; there is an element of Zelda Fitzgerald about her, Zelda who sought expression in writing, ballet, and painting in competition with Scott, but also simply for self-expression.

David and Catherine find secluded beaches where they can swim and tan in the nude. Catherine seeks to be the darkest white woman ever, in small part to be like the African girls she presumes David knew, but primarily as self-expression—she will be her own work of art—and as a sign of her personal darkness. She has her hair cut as short as a boy's, saying, "I'm a girl. But now I'm a boy too, and I can do anything and anything and anything." She is androgynous, and that night insists that she is Peter and he is Catherine. "Will you change and be my girl and let me take you?" she says, and sodomizes him with her finger.

They visit Madrid—and the Prado—then on to La Naupole on the Riviera. Catherine continues to lighten her hair and insists that David bleach his as well. He acquiesces and then must admit to himself that he likes it. Hemingway was a hair fetishist. One can see it in his novels, starting with Brett's hair cut short like a boy's, to when Catherine says that if Henry grew his hair longer, "I could cut mine and we'd be alike only one of us blonde and one of us dark." Later, he is aroused when she gets a permanent. Maria, in *For Whom the Bell Tolls*, has short hair after having her head shorn and says, "neither one can tell that one of us is one and not the other.... I would be thee because I love thee so." Whether this hair fetishism arose from weak gender identity as a result of being twinned with his sister is a matter of ongoing speculation, but it's definitely present in his fiction.

David and Catherine meet a lesbian couple, one of whom, Marita, is attracted to Catherine. Soon thereafter, Catherine brings Marita back to the couple's hotel to form a *ménage à trois*, having sex with Marita and then turning her over to David. In Catherine and David's relationship, she insists increasingly on being male. To feel represented, Catherine wants David to write their story, an account of their ongoing honeymoon. He does so, but then interrupts it to write stories of Africa, of his father's involvement in the Maji-Maji Rebellion, and of a hunt for an elephant with huge tusks. David shares these stories with Marita, whom he grows to love, as Catherine acts increasingly irrational.

The main African story, developed in separate chapters of *Garden*, was published by itself in *Sports Illustrated* in 1986 and in the Finca Vigia edition of the short stories. It tells of young David, out hunting with his dog at night, who sees a large elephant whose tusks reach nearly to the ground. David tells his father, who, with an African companion Juma, set out the next day to hunt the elephant for his tusks, for the money they will bring, meaning alcohol and women; David's mother never appears or is mentioned. It becomes an arduous trek; the elephant is going to an elephant graveyard to visit a companion killed in the past by Juma.

David associates with the elephant. It becomes a totem animal for him, and he regrets ever having told his father about it. "Juma will drink his share of the ivory or just buy himself another goddamn wife." Further, he decides, "I'm going to keep everything a secret always.... Never tell anyone anything ever. Never tell anyone anything again." A strange resolution for a novelist. He also announces to his father, "Fuck elephant hunting." When the elephant is killed, "all the dignity and majesty and all the beauty was gone from the elephant and he was a huge wrinkled pile." Death is an ever-present theme in Hemingway's works. And David concludes, "[t]he elephant was his hero now as his father had been for a long time.... [It was] the beginning of the knowledge of loneliness."

The story completed, Catherine, angry that David has abandoned their wedding narrative, burns his African stories—saving the story of the two of them, in which she finds expression. She leaves David and Marita, going to Paris, where she will ask appraisers to value David's African stories so that she can reimburse him for them, and where she can get Picasso, Pascin (Scribners misspells it as Pacsen) Derain, and Dufy to illustrate the wedding story. David tries to rewrite what Catherine has burned and initially fails. But lovemaking with warm, understanding, supportive Marita cures him, and the next day in the published text he can remember one of the African stories completely and write it better than before. The novel ends with David, his craft intact, with a better understanding of his father—as Nick also had in "Fathers and Sons"—united with Marita, whose name is very close to forms of "marriage" in English, French, or Italian. Marita is one of those women whom Hemingway invented as too good to be true: beautiful, rich, multilingual, more womanly than Catherine (by her own claim), a better wife (as Catherine admits), and understanding of David's work, which she has read before they met and is not threatened by it as Catherine is. She abandons lesbianism for presumably faithful heterosexuality as easily as David abandons Catherine. Her character and role, and David's easy ability to remember and rewrite his stories are the hardest things to credit in this crafted-by-editorial hands novel.

There had been lesbianism in Hemingway's writings before, in "Mr. and Mrs. Elliott" and in "The Sea Change," as well as in *Moveable Feast*. Male homosexuality is in "A Simple Enquiry" (*In Our Time*) "The Mother of a Queen" (*Winner Take Nothing*), and *To Have and Have Not*. The gender fluidity expressed in *Garden* did much to reduce Hemingway's hyper-masculine image, reduced charges of misogyny, and introduced whole new areas of criticism.

The African Book

Accounts of the African safari that Ernest and Mary took in 1953-54 first saw print in a *Look* magazine article in January 1954. It had been dictated in Nairobi in January as Ernest was recovering from the two plane crashes and was accompanied by photos taken by Earl Thiesen. Among the photos was one of Ernest beside a leopard that had originally been wounded by Mayito Menacal, a Cuban friend who had accompanied the Hemingways on the early part of the safari. Since Menocal had shot it first, it was his leopard, and Hemingway felt that he had to shoot another leopard before the picture was published or he was taking credit for something not his. Hemingway worked on the text from late 1954 until February 1956, when he put aside the manuscript—which ends in mid-sentence—to work on filming *The Old Man and the Sea*. He never returned to it.

The next appearance was in three installments in *Sports Illustrated* in 1971-72. Third, much of Hemingway's manuscript appeared in son Patrick's *True at First Light*, an abbreviated version of what Hemingway had written. The title Patrick had taken came from the line: "In Africa a thing is true at first light and a lie by noon and you have no more respect for it than for the lovely, perfect weed-fringed lake you see across the sun-baked plain." This may be Patrick's delicate way of saying that some of what his father wrote is exaggerated or a mirage. The final version, *Under Kilimanjaro*, is a scholarly edition by Robert Lewis and Robert Fleming, with limited scholarly apparatus. They include a brief introduction, a list of characters, less complete than Patrick's, and without his personal comments, and a glossary, again, less complete than Patrick's, who, with years as a white hunter and farmer in Tanganyika, knows Swahili. What they add is very brief textual notes where Hemingway had written in margins "Fix this" or left blanks to fill in later, or left out a word or more that obscured meaning; they do not translate Hemingway's French or, except in one instance, identify references.

Under Kilimanjaro, much like *Hills of Green Africa*, is an almost diary-like account of Ernest and Mary's days in a safari camp on the southern border of Kenya. It covers the latter part of the safari, after hunts near Magadi with Philip Percival, who had come out of retirement to lead the Hemingways' safari. The early part of the book also covers part of the Mau Mau rebellion in East Africa, an attempt by the indigenous people to wrest control from colonial forces, here, the British. The core of the Mau Mau movement were members of the Kikuyu tribe, while where the Hemingways were located were primarily Masai and Wakamba tribal lands. To counteract the loss of tourism that fear of the Mau Mau had caused, the British government in Kenya made celebrity Hemingway an Honorary Game Warden, with duties to eliminate animals that preyed on native flocks or people, protect elephants unless they trampled fields or people, and administer first aid to the natives.

A group of Mau Maus had escaped from where they had been detained and were heading toward the Hemingways' location; thus Ernest is concerned with gathering information as to their movements from those in the nearest town sympathetic to their cause, while also seeing to the defense of his camp, a likely target because of its guns and ammunition. He also has to see that Mary gets her lion. She was supposed to have killed a lion before, but Ernest wasn't sure that the one they saw was the one accused of predating, and so prevented her; she's also hampered by her short height, too short to see over the tall grass. And Ernest has to find and kill a leopard before the year is over. All of this occupies his musings, as well as—simultaneously—frequent protestations of affection for Mary while conducting his flirtation with Debba, a Wakamba girl.

Debba's attraction to Hemingway is easily explained. He is a wealthy, powerful man, and she lives on a dirt-poor farm with no cattle, the standard measure of wealth. His attraction to her is harder to explain. He obviously responds to her attentiveness to him. She is the young object of infatuation between Adriana Ivancich and Valerie Danby-Smith. Hemingway describes Debba as young and beautiful; Denis Zaphiro, the Kenyan Game Ranger under whom

Hemingway worked, described her as a "slovenly looking brat with a primitive greedy face. She was also none too clean." Mary was not threatened. She told Ernest that if he wanted a second wife, it was all right with her, but first, that Debba should have a bath.

Only once does Hemingway write that he went to bed with Debba, and then informs us that the bed, afterward, was broken. This event occurred the night before Mary returned from Nairobi, where she had gone for treatment of dysentery and to buy Christmas presents. The night of her return, Hemingway boasts that they made love three times—without breaking the bed.

The book has some lovely descriptions of the country but is mostly interior monologue or reported conversations with Mary, Game Rangers, his troop of employees, and a drunken Masai, called the Informer who lives in the nearby village and brings him information. Hemingway denounces his own earlier practice, during the 1933-34 safari, of calling the African men "boys," and makes a concerted effort to recognize the Africans who work for him as people with rights, their own histories, and dignity. He jokes with them, in his limited Swahili, and shares bottles of beer with them, passing the bottle back and forth. In fact, he makes a concerted effort to go native, and perhaps the relationship with Debba was part of that. He shaves his head, dyes his clothes the rusty color of Masai clothing, and hunts alone at night, armed only with a spear. There is a connection here to Catherine Bourne tanning her skin dark and David Bourne getting into his father's mind to write his African stories during this same period of the mid-fifties.

As I said, the African journal ends in mid-sentence; Hemingway never polished it into a more cohesive form, as he also never finished *Moveable Feast*, the Sea Book, or *The Garden of Eden*. And mental deterioration after the second plane crash made those tasks impossible. There are not likely to be more posthumous books, unless the heirs agree to an edition of the complete *Garden of Eden* manuscript.

10. Hemingway's Legacy

To repeat, Hemingway was a very complicated man, putting up a masculine front before a sensitive, essentially shy artist. Early on, the pose helped him sell books: he was not a long-haired, limp-wristed *artiste* but a man's man who wrote tough stories that could be read by the common reader, by men, when women then and now are the primary readers of fiction, more accessible in his simple prose than other Modernists such as Joyce and Faulkner. Literary critics could also appreciate him. But the macho pose hardened into a confining shell, and when it no longer fit the aging and infirm man, when he could no longer live up to it, and when his brain deteriorated to the extent that he could no longer write, he ended it; suicidal thoughts are replete in his letters throughout his lifetime.

The personal history is tragic. That the stigma against mental problems prevented him, in regard to his reputation, from seeking proper psychiatric help, is part of the tragedy—and is still today. But beyond the personal is the art, and he changed how English-language fiction was written in the twentieth century. He eschewed including every detail of description, every flick of an eyebrow or fan as late nineteenth, early twentieth-century authors did. Instead, he gave the essential facts of a situation, and only them—in his words, "the sequence of movement and fact that created the emotion"—in seemingly simple declarative sentences, leaving interpretation largely up to the reader. Those with different life experiences read the texts differently, saw different elements, responded differently. Those who had been to war read "Soldier's Home" very differently from those who had not. That also meant that as readers aged and acquired new experiences, their views of the stories could also change. One could come back to a story and find that it read differently. Without editorial comment, the stories show what happened and do not tell the reader how to respond. As

Aldous Huxley said of Hemingway's fiction, the meaning is all in the white spaces between the lines.

Hemingway and Fitzgerald made a pact never to end a story with a wow, with an O. Henry twist that reversed expectations and closed stories with a click. Instead, like Henry James before him, but in simpler prose, and like Chekov, Hemingway created scenes of everyday life—and death—with enormous psychological implications, and depended on his readers to discover and respond to those implications. It was an extreme show, don't tell. And Hemingway presented his lines in carefully crafted prose, with subtle alliterations and repetitions, prose poems, and even more subtle allusions so that those who recognize them have enriched readings. Nick in "Big-Two-Hearted River" is a returning war-scarred, psychologically damaged veteran seeking comfort in familiar things and a sense of control once again in his life. That he is also a Fisher King, wounded in a Waste Land of war, and simultaneously the questing knight seeking healing doesn't change the basic meaning; it simply enlarges it to give it historical and mythical proportion. Hemingway influenced widely disparate authors, with followers such as Raymond Carver, playwright Tom Stoppard (who began his literary career as a short story writer), and Cormac McCarthy. He influenced those who rebelled against him, such as Saul Bellow, who in his first novel, *Dangling Man*, railed against Hemingway and the "era of hard boileddom.... The hardboiled are compensated in their silence; they...fight bulls or catch tarpon." Nevertheless, Bellow created a protagonist in the image of macho, chest-beating Hemingway in *Henderson the Rain King*.

Hemingway's spare, sparse style did not last. It loosened in *A Farewell to Arms* and still more in subsequent books, returning in *The Old Man and the Sea* and some of the episodes in *A Moveable Feast*. The content, however, remained largely the same. Most people do not get all they want; they lose and are measured by the substance of their character in loss and defeat. It is an Existential situation, a matter of choice. How we define ourselves, and whether we live with those definitions also measures us, whether bullfighters like Manuel Garcia, boxers like Jack Brennan, game hunters in *Green Hills of Africa* or *Under Kilimanjaro*, partisan fighters like Robert Jordan, or fishermen like Santiago; do we live by our own codes? We all die. How we prepare for that eventuality, and how much we live joyously in the present that we have, is also a measure of each of us.

Hemingway was the most famous, most photographed writer of the twentieth century. That fame ultimately overcame him. It created a persona he could no longer live up to; he never could, but when young, he came closer. He survived near death in World War I, being blown up by a trench mortar, survived World War II and two plane crashes, but then deteriorated under different impediments. He may well have had PTSD and was tormented by insomnia and bad dreams for the rest of his life. His most insidious detriment, however, was the mental disease he inherited from his father, never properly diagnosed, most likely a form of depression, possibly bi-polar, that he self-medicated with drink. Near the end of his life, his son Patrick called him a "quart-a-day" drinker. That caused a second disease, alcoholism. The third disease was chronic traumatic encephalopathy from the number of concussions he sustained. The last one, from the plane crash in Butiaba, Uganda, was severe and hastened his decline, and he never completed a book-length manuscript after it. He took multiple drugs and supplements, including testosterone, Reserpine, Doriden (a sedative), Equanil (the tranquilizer Miltown), massive doses of vitamins A and B, Seconal (a barbiturate) to sleep, and Ritalin to wake up. How these drugs interacted with each other, and with the alcohol he drank, I am not qualified to say, but they could not have been healthy. His treatment at the Mayo Clinic, electroshock therapy, destroyed his short-term memory and the material that enabled him to write, rather than giving him anti-psychotic medications then on the market, such as Thorazine, and in so doing destroyed his reason for living. He defined himself as a writer, and he no longer could.

Nevertheless, from 1923 until his death in 1961, 38 years,

Hemingway produced two early chapbooks, four volumes of short stories, five novels and one novella, a non-fiction account of an African hunt, as well as a treatise on bullfighting: fourteen books, plus copious amounts of journalism, and drafts of unfinished books that would be published in six more volumes, while also covering two major conflicts, the Spanish Civil War and World War II. His poetry has also been collected. When not writing for commercial publication, he was a compulsive letter writer, and Oxford University Press is collecting his letters in 17 volumes; five have already been published, and they give an account of his daily life more so than his biographies; I would have said "an unfiltered account" or "a more truthful account," but that would not be true. He always wrote with the letter's recipient in mind, tailoring his accounts and his language to them. As he said, "all writers of fiction are liars," and there is lying and fiction in his letters.

He died too young at 61 and badly broken, but he exhibited an amazing midwestern, Protestant work ethic that turned out copious amounts of material that document his life and over half a century of the western world. And with his sparse, declarative sentences, and with his insistence that an active life—such as war or fishing—could be as much a source of fine literature as the parlor or drawing-room, he changed literature forever, not just in America.

Suggested Reading

There is a Hemingway industry; books proliferate by the month. This week alone there have been two new books, a picture book and a translation of a Spanish text. To begin with biographies, the basic and still very useful one is Carlos Baker's 1969 *Hemingway: A Life Story*. It was followed by Michael Reynolds' 5-volume version, Scott Donaldson's (1977), Jeffrey Meyers (1985), Kenneth Lynn (1987), and James Mellow (1992), among the more reliable ones. More recently, there have been newer accounts by James Hutchison (2016), Verna Kale (2016), and Mary Dearborn (2017). There have been memoirs, Mary Hemingway's *How It Was* (1976), A. E. Hotchner's *Papa Hemingway* (1983), and Marcelline Hemingway Sanford's *At the Hemingways* (1999), as well as ones by siblings Leicester, Sunny, and Madelaine, and one by son Gregory. William White edited a collection of his non-fiction pieces for the Toronto *Star Weekly*, *Esquire*, *PM*, and *Collier's*, *By-Line: Ernest Hemingway* (1967). More focused, less comprehensive accounts are *The Apprenticeship of Ernest Hemingway* (1954) by Charles Fenton; *Hemingway's Craft* by Sheldon Norman Grebstein (1973); *Hemingway's Nick Adams* by Joseph M. Flora (1982); *The Hemingway Women* by Bernice Kert (1983); *Hemingway in Love and War*, by Henry S. Villard and James Nagel (1989); *Hemingway in Italy and Other Essays*, edited by Robert W. Lewis (1990); *Ernest Hemingway* by Peter Messent (1992); *Hemingway Repossessed*, edited by Kenneth Rosen (1994); *The Cambridge Companion to Ernest Hemingway*, edited by Scott Donaldson (1996); *French Connections*, edited by J. Gerald Kennedy and Jackson R. Bryer (1998); *All Man* by David M. Earle (2009); *Hemingway's Boat* (2011) by Paul Hendrickson; *Hotel Florida* (2014) by Amanda Vaill; *The Breaking Point: Hemingway, Dos Passos, and the Murder of Jose Robles*, by Stephen Koch (2012); *The Ambulance Drivers* by James McGrath Morris (2017); and *Writer, Sailor, Soldier,*

Spy: Ernest Hemingway's Secret Adventures, 1935-1961 by Nicholas Reynolds (2018).

Books dealing specifically with Hemingway's sexuality are Mark Spilka's *Hemingway's Quarrel with Androgyny* (1990), Comley and Scholes' *Hemingway's Genders*, (1994), Carl Eby's *Hemingway's Fetishism* (1999), Debra Moddelmog's *Reading Desire* (1999), Richard Fantina's *Ernest Hemingway: Machismo and Masochism* (2005). Picture books include Peter Buckley's *Ernest* (1978), A. E. Hotchner's *Hemingway and His World* (1989,), Boris Vejdovsky's and Mariel Hemingway's, *Hemingway: A Life in Pictures* (2011), and *Hidden Hemingway*, by Robert K. Elder, Aaron Vetch, and Mark Cirino (2016); two Cuban ones are *Hemingway: Poor Old Papa* by Claudio Izquierdo Funcia (1995) and *Ernest Hemingway Rediscovered* by Roberto Herrera Sotolongo and Norberto Fuentes (1988).

Kent State University Press has published two series of books on Hemingway. There is the *Teaching Hemingway* series, with individual volumes of collected essays on teaching *The Sun Also Rises, For Whom the Bell Tolls*, the *Short Stories, Hemingway and Gender, Hemingway and War, Hemingway and Race, Hemingway and Modernism, Hemingway and the Natural World*, and *Hemingway in the Digital Age*. Another series is the *Reading Hemingway* series, line-by-line annotations, and commentary on his texts. So far there are *Reading* The Sun Also Rises, *Reading* A Farewell to Arms, *Reading* To Have and Have Not, *Reading* Across the River and into the Trees, *Reading* The Old Man and the Sea, *Reading* Men Without Women, *Reading* Winner Take Nothing, with *Reading* The Garden of Eden forthcoming.

In *Death in the Afternoon*, Hemingway derided, no doubt out of envy, Faulkner's productivity in the early 1930s: "You can't go wrong on Faulkner. He's prolific too. By the time you get them ordered, there'll be new ones out." The same can be said about books on Hemingway.

About the Author

Peter L. Hays is professor emeritus of English at the University of California, Davis, from 1966 to 2004. A noted Hemingway scholar, he is the editor of *Teaching Hemingway's* The Sun Also Rises (2003) and author of *A Concordance to Hemingway's* In Our Time (1990), *The Critical Reception of Hemingway's* The Sun Also Rises (2011), and *Fifty Years of Hemingway Criticism* (2013).

A Word from the Publisher

Thank you for reading *Simply Hemingway*!

If you enjoyed reading it, we would be grateful if you could help others discover and enjoy it too.

Please review it with your favorite book provider such as Amazon, BN, Kobo, Apple Books, or Goodreads, among others.

Again, thank you for your support and we look forward to offering you more great reads.

Made in the USA
Las Vegas, NV
17 December 2021

38155703R00080